STORKED!

A MEMOIR

adoption secrecy and
the search for identity

K. C. Sanford

Storked!

Published by The Breathing Room

For more information, visit kcsanford.com

ISBN: 979-8-9853914-2-8

First Edition

For dad,

the one who gave me life,

and the one that made my life possible

STORKED:

Verb. When a couple has an unwanted pregnancy occur.

-Urban Dictionary

AUTHOR'S NOTE

Adoptees are unique. Not all of our stories are the same, and our adoption experiences affect us differently. This book is about my journey to find my birth parents and how the closed adoption system threatened my sense of identity. Events have been reconstructed based on my memory, notes, and the memories of others. Third-person dialogue depicts scenes that only one person could substantiate, and some of this narrative relied on my imagination for story development. Please fault closed adoption secrecy for any discrepancies. There are no composite characters, and names, when used, have not been altered—apart from one, mine. The author that appears on the front cover is a meld of names that I have had during my life. I use K. C. Sanford as a way to protect the anonymity of those who appear within these pages. You want to know who I am. I truly understand. To you, I say, welcome to my world.

CONTENTS

Prologue

PROLOGUE

Believe nothing you hear, and only one half that you see.

"The System of Dr. Tarr and Prof. Fether"
-Edgar Allan Poe, writer, poet, orphan

The message took me five minutes to write and five times as long to send. My finger hovered over the mouse, knowing my life was about to change. *Are you absolutely sure you want to do this?*

Four days earlier, I received my DNA results from one of those cheap, spit-in-a-tube ancestry kits. I had expected another dead end, but—six weeks later—the results revealed a close family match. A first cousin. A female.

I scoured the internet for any information I could find about this first cousin stranger, but her name was too common to be helpful. If there was any hope of answering the question that's been knocking around in my head for so long, I had to reveal myself. *Would she know who I was before I was Kacie?*

I clicked *send.*

Less than twelve hours later, I received a message in return. "Hello! Yes, I know EXACTLY who you are!!"

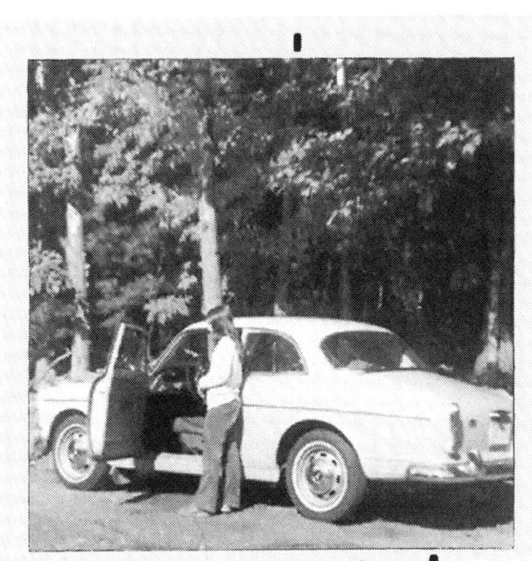

Assimilate

ASSIMILATE

Birth Father

A pregnant girlfriend, reason enough to get out of town.

As he drove, he tried to push away the thought of his girlfriend being sent away to Florida. How had they gotten to this point?

The plan was to pick up his friend Ray at the naval base in Boston and head directly over to the enlisted men's club a few blocks away. Ray was a friend from high school who joined the military shortly after graduation. When Ray called out of the blue earlier that week, he wasn't surprised. Their girlfriends were best friends, and he figured that Ray had heard about the pregnancy. Ray must have known that he needed a good distraction and called to invite him down for the weekend.

As he pulled up to the base's dormitory quarters, he noticed Ray already walking toward him. He was late, and he knew his friend must be eager to get to the club because Ray opened the passenger door to get in before the car was out of gear. Ray directed him to the club and into the already packed parking lot. It was Friday, the night when the locals came in, so he slid his two-door coupe into a space as close to the club's entrance as possible.

Before heading inside, they sat in the car, getting caught up over a shared joint that had traveled with him in the coupe's ashtray. It didn't take too long for Ray to ask the question that he knew was on the tip of his friend's tongue since he got into the car, "What's going to happen with the baby?"

Birth Mother

Auntie Tilly met her at the airport. It was still cold when she left Logan Airport, and the warm, humid air felt good as she stepped off the plane. Picking up her small suitcase, she suddenly realized how little she brought for an extended stay. She had struggled to pack for the radical change in weather and her expanding waistline.

Before leaving the airport, Tilly mentioned that she had found a private adoption agency. "Call them," she said. "You should make an informed decision about the baby, and meeting with an adoption agency can help."

Auntie Tilly wasn't her actual aunt by blood. She was the beloved second wife of her uncle, and she had always considered Tilly her aunt—her favorite aunt. Her compassion wasn't surprising. Tilly was a nurse. When she pleaded with her mom before her departure to let her keep the baby, it was made clear that adoption was her only choice. She spent the entire flight thinking about her baby's father. Without him, adoption was the only option. *Wasn't it?*

She arrived in Florida feeling dejected, and in two words, Auntie Tilly managed to change all that. *Informed decision.*

When they pulled out of the airport, she felt the intense sun hit her face. She dug through her pocketbook for her sunglasses. As she put them on, she thought about the possibilities. Maybe she could keep her baby. Perhaps Auntie Tilly would help her.

ONE

I was born when I was nine days old.

Looking down at the piece of paper that stated almost as much, I stepped up to the worn brown laminate counter and slid my application across to the woman with the no-nonsense face. "You forgot something," she said almost immediately, pointing to the line that said: *Place of Birth*. "What city were you born in?"

I came armed with a stock answer, but the words wouldn't leave my lips. My body wouldn't cooperate. Like a dog's tail, my face was my tell, and just then, all my blood rushed my face. No-nonsense face tapped the omission a couple of times with her finger. Embarrassed, I finally said, "I don't know where I was born. I was adopted."

Twenty minutes earlier, I'd arrived at the county courthouse to apply for my first passport. The entrance of the 1918 Neoclassical building—designed with four massive columns, each topped with Ionic capitals supporting one large stone pediment chiseled with the court's name—had been imposing. For me, this court building was the place where my familial ties were both severed and formed, the place where my true identity was locked away and replaced with a new one, the place where my adoption was finalized sixteen years earlier, and the place where, years later, I asked a judge to unseal my adoption records. But at that moment, it stood as the place that prevented the certification of my identity so that I could leave the country. How can one building have so much power?

I was four when my parents first told me I was adopted.

"Kacie," my dad said, "we have something very important to tell you." My brother and I were summoned to the living room moments earlier, and we were now sitting on the dull green shag carpeting, looking up at our parents as they sat on the slate stairs leading into the sunken room. I thought I was in trouble for some act I couldn't remember committing—the living room, usually off-limits, except for special occasions. *Maybe*, I thought, *they're using it as a place to give out punishments now too.* My brother put a reassuring arm around me.

I looked over my shoulder at the large piece of art on the dark paneled wall to see if it was out of place. It was a bunch of colorful squares and lines that my mom said had been painted by her artist friend Judy who had also painted a picture of my brother on the wall in our dining room. Earlier, the brightly colored painting and the even brighter couch had called to me like beacons of adventure. They were hard to resist as I walked by on my way to my bedroom, and I'd had a little jump session on the couch even though I knew I shouldn't have. *Maybe I bumped the painting? Maybe she found out about that one time I'd licked the couch, thinking it would taste as good as it looked?* Lost in thought, I heard my dad say, "You were adopted."

I turned and stared at him wide-eyed and asked, "What does that mean?"

He said, "It means that you didn't grow inside mommy's belly."

My mom then placed her hand on her stomach and added, "You didn't grow inside here like your brother Danny."

My dad went on to say, "You grew inside of another lady's belly. She loved you very much but couldn't take care of you because she was too young."

That's when Jeff chimed in, "I was adopted too. It makes us very special." And at that moment, I felt very special.

My dad is a great storyteller. His lead-in of "stop me if you heard this before" is usually met with silence by me. Not because he hadn't told the story. I have heard all of his stories many times over, and I always want to listen to them again. His subtle changes in character expressions or the order of events always breathe new life into his old tales. And only my dad could survive the incidents he describes—being shot in the back with an arrow while target shooting with his friend Ralph, having a friend accidentally drop an ax on his head while climbing up into a treehouse, or playing chicken with a train.

The fact that I remember my adoption story the way I do makes me not trust the memory. It doesn't seem possible to be that young and recall something so vivid. In my version of events, I remember my dad being matter-of-fact. There were no exciting character expressions. There was no storytelling. When I asked him about that time in the living room later as I grew up, he said he didn't remember my version or anything specific about that day. It was a life-altering moment for me, and yet my dad seemed out of character. He craved a good story to tell. But he was not the star in this tale, and I later learned that my parents didn't have much of anything to disclose. I had to script my own narrative, filling in a void so large it seemed to swallow my identity wholesale—from nothing, I had to craft something, and that something happened to be all of me.

My parents met in college and moved from the Midwest to Florida in 1965, shortly after they married. They settled into their new suburban lives and tried to start a family without much success. Doctors didn't know why my parents couldn't conceive, and in the 1960s, there wasn't much anyone could do to help the natural process. Their attempts at artificial insemination had failed, and the first baby to be born through in vitro fertilization was still more than a decade away. They were surrounded by family and friends starting to have children, and their desire to build a family grew. Parenthood, after all, was seen as a requirement for a successful marriage.[1]

In 1968, good friends of my parents were in the process of completing their second adoption. Seeing adoption as a possible way to build their family, my parents asked them about their experiences. Adoption was not a new concept. The dawn of modern adoption in the United States began in 1851 when Massachusetts passed the *Adoption of Children Act,* and the period between 1945 and 1973 signified a record number of babies surrendered by unmarried white women for adoption. My parents became one of many infertile couples who turned to adoption.[2]

While adoption was becoming a more acceptable form of building a family, my parents chose to tell only a few trusted friends and family members about their decision. My mom wanted her adopted child to be accepted as if she gave birth to him herself, and she requested a blue-eyed, blond-haired baby boy that would look like her. The adoption agency granted her wish, and in May 1969, they brought home my brother Jeff.

In August 1970, my parents returned to the adoption agency to apply for their second adoption, this time a baby girl. They were assigned the same social worker as their first adoption. Charlotte was a single, middle-aged woman who was always impeccably dressed. Her smile matched her optimism, and her soothing nature made for a good adoption social worker.

At their intake meeting, Charlotte gently informed my parents that fewer available children meant a longer waiting period for this adoption. She also told them that the agency no longer matched babies with their adoptive parents based on physical attributes and birth parent interests. Charlotte didn't elaborate on the agency's new thinking and philosophy; she only emphasized that they would not be sharing background information except for pertinent medical issues. These new policies were a drastic change from the adoption experience they'd had only two years earlier and one that caught my mom off guard. Charlotte noted in her record that my dad was in immediate agreement with the agency policy changes but that my mom needed reassurance and agreed only after a lengthy discussion.

While the entire process for my brother took nine months from application to baby, my parents waited a little over two years for me. In September 1972, they brought home a very cute, chubby-cheeked, baby girl with brownish-red hair, who they named Katherine and called Kacie—a baby that looked nothing like them.

Seven months after my parents brought me home, my mom was pregnant with my little brother Danny—her conception aligning with a recent trip to Spain with my dad. Her doctor surmised that reduced worry and stress around whether she could or would conceive may have contributed to her pregnancy. My theory, and the story I like to tell, is that Danny was my parent's tax for leaving their infant girl and young son behind while they traveled carefree in Europe.

My older brother and I were adopted during the tail end of what is referred to as the Baby Scoop Era.[3] This roughly thirty-year period between the end of World War II and the landmark U.S. Supreme Court decision of Roe v. Wade in 1973 marked a period of deliberate adoption secrecy. Prior to World War II, every effort was made to retain ties with the child's birth family. This philosophy was affirmed in the first set of adoption standards, *Minimum Safeguards in Adoption*, published by the Child Welfare League in 1938.[4]

The period after World War II marked a shift from traditional confidentiality, protecting records from the prying eyes of the public, to sealed secrecy by preventing members of the adoption triad (adoptee, birth parents, and adoptive parents) from accessing their adoption records and severing all biological ties. There are a few theories behind this move. Secrecy, social workers theorized, protected the adoptive family unit from a birth parent's change of heart. Secrecy also sought to protect the birth mother's privacy so she could better move on with her life and the childless couple from the shame of infertility.[5] My brother and I became part of the post-war closed adoption system, and the legal system permanently severed our biological connections.

When I went to the courthouse to apply for my passport, I brought the required birth certificate needed for identification. The United States began the formal process of issuing birth certificates at the turn of the twentieth century. When I was born in 1972, my birth was documented just like every other baby born that year. But I never left with that record of my birth because the hospital flagged me for adoption, and the courts sealed my original birth certificate along with my other adoption records. My birth certificate, the one that the passport clerk scrutinized to prove I was the person on the application form, was an amended version—an invention created to protect adopted children from the stigma of illegitimacy.[6] My amended birth certificate had blank spaces under the city and hospital of birth. The mother and father sections included my adoptive parent's information, and under the child's name was the name they gave me. It wasn't so much a record of my birth as a record of my adoptive identity—an identity I assumed nine days after being born.

My parents didn't leave the adoption agency with a how-to manual on raising adopted kids. Whenever they had questions, they turned to the family pediatrician for advice. Dr. Bennett was the one to tell them that my brother and I be told about our adoption sooner rather than later. She cautioned them that keeping our adoption status a secret would not lead to healthy outcomes. I couldn't grasp adoption secrecy's broader significance as a young child, but my pediatrician knew that keeping secrets from children was unhealthy. Still, the practice of severing all biological ties and concealing all evidence of an adopted child's former identity was the standard practice in the field of social work at that time. How were the two professionals tasked with my wellbeing seemingly siloed?

The answer may best be summarized by Karen Wilson Buterbaugh when she describes one of many defining conditions of the Baby Scoop Era:

> *The creation of a new professionalism in social work in the United States allowed workers to define and operate in the specialized field of infant adoption, regardless of their previous experience or training, and to declare themselves experts in unwed motherhood.*[7]

Charlotte was well-credentialed with a college degree in social work and a membership in the Academy of Certified Social Workers. But research and advocacy in actual adoptee outcomes didn't start until the 1970s, when adoptees and birth mothers began speaking out about their experiences. At the time of my adoption, nobody had checked in with adult adoptees to ask, "How do you feel about your adoption?" or "Based on your experience, how could the adoption process be improved?" Theories drove adoption policy, not outcomes.

My brother Jeff and I were the only adopted children in our extended family, and as a young child, I started to notice the similarities between family members. My younger brother, my parent's biological child, looked like them. My dad was an identical twin. My mom looked like her dad. My cousin Michelle, my maternal aunt's child, could have been my mom's biological daughter. It is human nature to talk about family resemblances, and our family was no different. But because I didn't look or act like anyone in our family, these discussions about resemblances always excluded me. I so desperately wanted to look like someone; I obsessed over it. When I couldn't see any similarities within my own family, I looked for my face in others—strangers out in public, teachers, friends, friends of friends. And yet, I was never made to *feel* adopted. My parents went out of their way to make sure they treated all their kids fairly; some might say, to a fault. We each got the same number of Christmas gifts each year. My parents equally divided their time between us and our activities. When one of us begged for a hamster, we all got hamsters. But there would always be a part of me missing, what my parents could never give me—the part of my identity I came by biologically.

Someone once told me that my biology doesn't need to dictate my biography, and I suppose it is easy to take for granted something you already have—knowledge of biological roots. How do you write a biography with an incomplete history? I didn't know where I got my curly hair, deep-set dimples, or natural athletic abilities. I couldn't complete the typical family tree school project. Am I considered English, like my dad, or Polish, like my mom, if I don't have their blood running through my veins? How does a severed branch of an unknown kind successfully graft itself onto a new tree?

The importance of biological ties is emphasized in the way adoptees are asked to affirm their place within a family—an affirmation not required of birth children.[8] Adoptees are treated as curiosities, and it is sometimes easier to avoid the topic of adoption altogether. If I let slip the fact that I was adopted, what I heard was, "Wow, I didn't know that you were adopted!" followed by all of the questions:

"Why did your real mom give you away?"

"How old were you when you were adopted?"

"Have you met your real parents?"

"Are you interested in finding your real parents?"

"Do you know anything about where you came from?"

"So, is that your real brother?"

"Couldn't your parents have children of their own?"

"When did your parents tell you that you were adopted?"

"Do you really feel like your adopted parents are your real parents?"

As intrusive as the questions felt, the use of the words "real" and "own" cut like a knife plunged deep into my heart. I have only physically known one set of parents. I can see them and touch them. If *real* implies "not artificial, fraudulent or illusory," then what are my parents to me?[9] My parents have three children, me and my two brothers. We have a "direct kinship," as the definition of *own* implies.[10] What other type of child could I be to my parents if not their own?

My experience getting grilled over my adoptee status is why I avoid asking strangers or new acquaintances probing questions. Admittedly, it's hard to suppress the urge to turn the proverbial tables and ask my series of questions.

"When your mom found out she was pregnant, or at any point since you've been born, did she think about giving you away?"

"Are you sure your parents are your real parents?"

"When did your parents tell you that you were their birth child?"

"Do you wish you were adopted?"

I eventually learned to accept my adoptee status as something I cannot change. If given the opportunity now, I will talk openly about my adoption experience, using it to educate others. But when tested, there is still a snarky reply at the ready—like when a stranger once approached me at a children's museum assuming that my daughter was adopted from a foreign country and asked how much she cost. My response: "Probably the same as it did to give birth to your daughter, except medical insurance didn't cover my experience."

My family is as real to me as yours is to you. I am my parent's own child. Many parts and experiences make me—some of which I know and others that I am not allowed to know because of adoption laws that make little sense to me. Why don't I have information regarding my *real* birth history? Because it is against the law for me to know my *own* birth history.

I don't remember asking many questions when my parents told me I was adopted. What would a four-year-old ask about something so complex? But as the years progressed, I'd ask more questions. *Where is my birth mother? What did she look like? Why was I given away? Why didn't she want me?* As hard as I pressed my parents for answers, they never had anything to offer. They left the adoption agency with their new baby girl and only three pieces of information about the birth mother.

She was eighteen. She was not married. There was a family history of diabetes.

The not knowing only made me more curious and anxious about the story nobody could tell. Having an older brother who was adopted was comforting to me, but he didn't share my need for answers. Maybe his lack of curiosity was because he knew more. The adoption agency gave my parents some information about his birth family and history. He knew the reason for his relinquishment—his birth parents were very young, at fifteen. They wanted to keep him but had no means to do so. They were in love. They were artistic. His paternal birth grandfather was a prominent realtor. My brother was also intentionally matched with my parents based on his birth parent's physical attributes and interests. He looked like my mom with her blond hair, and his thin frame was like my dad. He shared their blue eyes. His artistic talent (to match our mom) and his love of sailing (to match our dad) emerged as a young child. His story seemed straightforward and overwhelmingly positive. These reasons, and countless others, could have played a hand in curbing his appetite for information.

It is hard to understand the adoption agency's decision to place two children in one household in-between a significant shift in policy. And as a child, it was hard for me to understand why my brother came with a story and I did not. Maybe my story was one the social worker thought I'd be better off not knowing. I wonder if Charlotte thought much about the impact of one child having birth family information and parent similarities and the other one left to wonder.

Once asserting my adoption status across the counter that separated us, the clerk processed my application without further dialogue. I received a passport and chalked the experience up to one of many where I had to confront adoption identity head-on. But when I applied for my passport at age sixteen, this one experience coincided with a critical period of adolescence when teenagers attempt to resolve a fundamental question. *Who am I?*[11] For me, the context of my adopted life could only answer the question—a life developed solely by social relationships. The question of who I was became impossible for me to answer (at least not entirely) because I was so different from everyone else in my life.

Adoption is complicated. This book's cover is symbolic of what the closed adoption system was supposed to represent—the best solution to everyone's problem: an unwed pregnant teen, a parentless baby, the infertile couple willing to parent a stranger's child, and the sealing of all records so that everyone can just move on, always looking forward and never looking back. In the name of the child's best interest, love will conquer all. But love, I would come to find out, wasn't enough to answer one crucial question.

"Who am I?"

TWO

Here is what I think I know.

I was born to a young, unwed woman who gave me away because I wasn't good enough.

My mom's line of questioning had become our monthly ritual. "Kacie, what's wrong? Why aren't you dressed for school?" But my mom's tone was a bit different today, and I wondered if she had caught on. It was the third Tuesday of the month. Music class. The class where the teacher calls on you to answer questions about a specific musical instrument or, worse, makes you get up in front of the class to play a new instrument. I had to do that once when the teacher asked me to try the recorder. I brought the instrument to my lips and blew only to get a loud honking sound out of the other end. All my classmates saw my face turn bright red, and I wished I could have disappeared into the chalkboard behind me. It was awful.

I found my mom in the kitchen talking on the phone. She had the cord spiraled around her pointer finger when I came in, still dressed in my pajamas, and interrupted her conversation. I heard her say, "I'll call you back in a minute," before hanging up the wall phone to see why I wasn't dressed. "Kacie, we have to leave in ten minutes."

Only two years earlier, my parents requested a meeting with my first-grade teacher. I insisted that I was failing, and I wanted to prepare my parents before bringing my report card home. When Miss Mazda assured them that I was doing well, that I was, in fact, one of her best students, my parents were baffled. Their reassurance of how well I was doing did little to calm my anxiety.

This time I changed my approach—instead of talking about failing, I avoided all possible situations in which I could fail, like music class. This time, I pretended to be sick. I couldn't let anyone know that I was a horrible musician. I needed to be perfect.

"My stomach hurts." It was true. It felt funny. My mom seemed to believe my story because she put a reassuring arm around my shoulders and walked me back upstairs to my bedroom. Before tucking me into bed, she turned and left the room. I panicked, thinking she had caught onto my ruse, but she quickly returned with the yellow plastic bucket we kept under the bathroom sink across the hall and placed it next to my bed. "In case you need it," she said as she pulled my comforter from the foot of the bed and tucked it around my arms.

The bucket made sense. I did tell her my stomach didn't feel good, and I had earned the reputation of throwing up directly on the shaggy brown carpet next to my bed whenever I got sick in the middle of the night. I tried to defend myself, claiming that I couldn't make it to the bathroom in time. Truthfully, getting out of bed in the dark meant walking past the attic door that didn't fully latch. I was more afraid of what hid on the other side than angry parents forced to scrub barf out of the carpet.

If my mom was afraid of any potential mess now, it didn't show on her face. As she sat down next to me and began stroking my hair, I turned to look at the curtain covering the entire expanse of wall adjacent to my bed. My mom was always one step ahead of me. She had taken spare sheets and created a wall curtain because she was tired of seeing dirty footprints—I had a habit of sleeping with my feet propped on the wall, and I wasn't too keen on nightly baths. Now it was something I had to explain to friends who came over to play when they peeked behind to see what the curtain was hiding.

As I drifted off to sleep, my mom bent over, kissed my forehead, and said, "Maybe next month you can try that music class."

My mom stayed home with my brothers and me until we all reached elementary school, when she went back to work full-time. She asked Mrs. Williams, a retired woman on her bowling league team, if she would be interested in watching us after school. She politely declined, but my mom was never one to take no for an answer. It is hard to explain, but you just couldn't say no to my mom. Don't get me wrong, you would try, but you would always fail. She worked Mrs. Williams for a few weeks until she finally relented, on a trial period, just so my mom would stop asking. Yes, there were three of us, but my mom assured Mrs. Williams that her kids were terrific—well-behaved and responsible (as much as elementary-aged kids could be)—and that she'd be surprised if she didn't continue after the trial period.

I took to Mrs. Williams immediately. I like to think that our bond ultimately made her stay around for nearly six years, at which point we were all old enough to legally become latchkey kids, as my younger brother liked to call us. Mrs. Williams became another grandparent to me. I was a child who needed a lot of affection and reassurance, and she was more than willing to oblige. Mrs. Williams was both nurturing and firm, and I liked that about her. I snuggled up next to her and rubbed her arm like the silky edge of a security blanket. For a petite woman, she had a tremendous amount of arm flab that both fascinated and calmed me. I can still hear her laugh as she thanked me for drawing attention to her flabby flaw.

When I couldn't curl up next to someone, I resorted to sucking two fingers on my left hand for comfort. It must have bothered Mrs. Williams that I was still doing this at age seven, unlike my parents, who never said anything about my habit. Instead of confronting me, telling me I was too old for such things, she struck a deal when we were out shopping earlier that week, and she saw me stop to look at a cross pendant necklace. She said she'd buy the necklace and gift it to me when I stopped sucking my fingers. *Done*, I thought, and I was already imagining her presenting me with a small wrapped box. It was easy for me to stop once someone offered an incentive. Most finger-sucking moments came when I was lying down, and every time I had the urge to put my fingers in my mouth, I simply laid on my left hand. I really wanted that necklace! Within one week of seeing it for the first time, it was dangling around my neck. My finger-sucking days were over.

Mrs. Williams and I kept in touch until I was out of college and moved away from Florida. I still remember her feel, her smell, and that she always ordered a Manhattan when we got together for our annual lunch date. She never made me feel different, just special.

But as comfortable as I was with her in private, I became nervous every time we left the house. I feared being seen in public with her or anyone else who wasn't related to me. Described as an irrational fear by my parents, I can look back at this time in my life as my need to belong—my need to be with people who belonged to me.

My brothers and I all had a reason for attachment issues. My parents brought me home when I was nine days old. My older brother didn't come home for a full six weeks. He had been suffering from colic, and the adoption agency wanted to clear him medically before releasing him for adoption. My younger brother came home from the hospital without my mom after spending his first week in an incubator due to a heart defect. My mom became critically ill after having an emergency C-section for his birth, and she stayed in the hospital for four weeks. We all experienced trauma right after our birth, yet I was the only one who struggled.

I had a hard time being away from my family, and I constantly needed reassurance of being loved. My dad became concerned when, well past the age of four, I still needed him to carry me. He made another appointment with the family pediatrician for advice, and her solution was simple. *Just carry her. Eventually, she will get tired of it.* The pediatrician was right. By the time I reached the fourth grade, I had become more independent and didn't need as much attention from my parents.

It was hard to appease my need to belong and my need for reassurance. I felt loved. I felt supported. And yet I always found myself in a constant battle to prove that I was worthy of living the life I was given. For me, being adopted was exhausting.

I wasn't encouraged to talk about my adoption or its effects on my life. Everyone, including my parents, thought (or at least acted like) it was no big deal. They were giving me a great life filled with opportunities. It was the same life they gave my baby brother, their biological child. Were we not the same? Almost. If my younger brother failed, my parents had only themselves to blame. It was, after all, their blood and their parenting that made Danny, Danny. If I failed, could my parents blame my faulty genetic material? Could they blame me? Could they send me back if I wasn't perfect? I couldn't be unborn, but could I be unadopted? My birth mother already gave me away.

THREE

I got into his white truck without saying a word. I already felt uncomfortable, and the striped knit seat cover itching the back of my legs was not helping. It had been two years since the initial incident. My parents had agreed to host our year-end soccer party because we had a pool. For a bunch of middle schoolers, having a pool party was still appealing.

He was the only adult to swim, the others mingling on the nearby screened porch. He stood chest-high near the pool's perimeter and watched as his team of girls played pool tag. I was underwater evading capture, when I felt a hand slip up my bathing suit and squeeze my butt. Pressing my foot off the bottom of the pool, I rose out of the water to find myself looking at him and the smirk forming on his face.

I don't remember ever liking him. When I joined the soccer team as an elementary-aged girl, his wife was the coach. He took over as we entered middle school and into the top tier of play for our region and age bracket. He was a good coach, and we were a good team. But I didn't like his stern attitude or his lack of empathy for coaching girls. While our bodies grew and changed, he worked chest trapping drills into every practice. And then there were the nonchalant breast brushes, inappropriate slaps on the "back."

I avoided him as much as I could, and I made a point never to be alone with him. But being alone with him became inevitable one day when nobody was available to drive me to practice. If I missed practice for no good reason, I couldn't play in the next game. That was the rule, and I loved soccer more than anything. When my mom told me that he'd be bringing me to practice, I threw a teen temper tantrum. She took it as a spoiled girl maneuver and nothing more. My dad was out of town, and she told me that she couldn't accommodate everyone's schedule all at once. I don't remember what was on her calendar for that afternoon, but my soccer practice had moved to the bottom of the list.

I couldn't tell my parents about my coach's behavior. It meant losing my chance to play on one of the best teams in our area. My parents couldn't commit to driving me much further away to another team while managing their careers and two other children. I knew that. So I took the coach grabs as part of the game I was playing. And now I was trapped with him, alone. He tried to make small talk as I pressed against the passenger door. At a stoplight, he pulled out a bag of nuts and started eating. He said, "I hope I don't grab the wrong one," when one dropped into his lap.

I dealt with my coach's sexual advances in my way. I made fun of him to my teammates, his tight baseball shorts, his ink-black goatee. I developed an attitude. As the team's leading goal scorer, I figured there was nothing I could do that would get me kicked off the team. I was right, but he retaliated. Predators seem to know what trait to exploit, and he fed on my need for perfection. At first, it was subtle—nitpicking everything I did or didn't do privately. Then it became more overt—publicly nitpicking everything I did or didn't do. Soon positive praise became nonexistent. I couldn't do anything right.

Once I reached high school, I played on the varsity soccer team during my club's off-season. This team's coach was positive and encouraging. It became a much-needed break, and my self-worth slowly started to shore itself up. And one night, when I saw my club coach sitting in the stands, I played one of my best games.

I had assumed he came to watch a couple of his players in a high school match. Most of my club team went to a different school except Kelly and me. She lived around the corner, and we had been playing club soccer together for five years. The two of us made a dominating offensive line on both teams—her as center mid and me as left-wing. After the game, our coach approached us with the exciting news that our club team would play in an elite spring tournament. When I asked him more about the upcoming game, he said, "Kacie, you're not playing in the tournament. I didn't put you on the roster." Beneath his serious tone, I could see that same smirk smile he flashed in the pool. He thought nothing of announcing this in front of my teammate and our moms, who'd come to watch us play.

My heart sank. Before I could react, my mom said, "You are an awful person. Coming here to my daughter's game and telling her that. You don't deserve to have her." She turned and walked away, and I was grateful to follow in her wake.

That spring, my mom made arrangements for me to try out for a different team three towns over. I made the team. And so did Kelly, who came with me to tryouts. When our new team played opposite our old squad and crushed them, I smiled.

There was never any doubt that my mom would step in front of a bus if it meant saving my life. We were nothing alike, and she loved me fiercely anyway. Our bond was a frayed rope that could give way at any moment. Her love came with conditions, and when tested, as children are wont to do, I knew that rope would unravel and snap. So, I yielded. I changed. I adapted. I consciously eased the tension on the threads that held us together. She demanded perfection, which meant being beautiful like she was beautiful and high achieving. And I tried. I couldn't have her blue eyes, but I was naturally athletic, which, at least, made my curvy frame fit. I wasn't book smart, but I could work extra hard to bring home As. I couldn't paint like her, but I was creative.

My dad was better at molding the best possible me. Maybe it was easier to see himself in me—we had exceptional mechanical abilities, were quick taskmasters, and enjoyed helping others. And though we had all these same things in common, he struggled to understand my lack of passion for things important to him.

Maybe conditional love and the internal struggle for acceptance happens in all families. Perhaps every child must adapt to fit in, adopted or not. And yet, I couldn't feel comfortable in my adoptive skin because it was what made me different. And feeling like critical pieces of my identity were missing made it even harder for me. Adapting couldn't fundamentally change who I was. I stood out, and I couldn't explain why. My differences more than outnumbered my similarities, and I was getting swallowed up by the void they created.

Being adopted himself, my brother Jeff made for a good ally growing up, and he helped me feel less out of place. It was two adopted children to one biological child, and we had the advantage. We teased our younger brother mercilessly about not being adopted. "Mom and dad picked us out, and they got stuck with you," was our favorite go-to line. We told him that he was the accident even after Jeff and I became old enough to understand that it was us who were truly not planned. Danny was a sensitive child, a trait we exploited, and Jeff and I take credit for his success in life by helping him develop his thick skin. We were siblings, but Danny stood out as being different from us. We were equals in every way but one—Danny wasn't adopted. Our need to point out Danny's difference most likely stemmed from the desire to affirm our natural place within an unnatural family construct. If we all felt different, we could all be the same.

When new people saw the three of us together, you could see their facial expressions shift as they tried to figure us out—furrowed brows seemingly asking the question, *I know they are siblings, but why don't they look like siblings?* One of his college friends saw the three of us sitting together at Danny's wedding and approached to ask, "Danny, were you adopted?" Raising her finger to point back and forth between Jeff and me, she said, "You two look so much like your parents. Where did you come from, Danny?" All we could do was laugh.

My parents waited until they were officially approved to adopt a baby before telling family and close friends about their plans, surprised by the overwhelmingly positive support once the news broke. Super 8 video from our early years captures happy moments, smiling faces, and a loving grandma holding me. No one was the wiser that she saw her adopted and biological grandchildren differently.

My maternal grandparents bought a condo in Florida and migrated south every winter from Ohio to be closer to their grandchildren and the warmer weather—we lived on the same coast, and my cousins lived four hours away on the other. My grandpa adored me. My grandma, not so much. No one picked up on her hints of dissatisfaction that I felt through her actions—like how she consistently misspelled my name using a "y" instead of an "ie." I remember a time bounding through the door of her condo with my arms outstretched for a hug, only to be greeted with a shove to the side. "I already hugged you, Kacie," she grunted in her raspy smoker's voice while pushing me away and walking past me to hug my cousins. Confused, I walked to the back of the line waiting for my turn for a hug that never came. I hadn't seen my grandparents for a couple of days, but my cousins were visiting from out of town, and she hadn't seen them for a couple of months. My grandma only had so many hugs to give, and I had already used my allotment.

She doted on my two cousins and Danny probably because they looked like her Polish ancestors. She attended all their weddings but didn't make an appearance at mine or Jeff's ceremonies. Being adopted meant being different, and not everyone appreciates differences.

My mother-in-law was more overt with her feelings about adoption. When my husband and I decided to adopt a baby, we planned a trip to tell his parents in person. Our excitement was met with a pursed face and the statement, "Having your own children would be best." Best? What did she mean? She knew that I was adopted, and now she seemed to question my goodness. Love was supposed to conquer all. Adoptees are supposed to be blank slates ready to be molded by new families. But even my mother-in-law knew that we came with unknown baggage. She was just being honest about it.

I can't change someone's investment in biological ties or any negative feelings attached to adoption. I focused on my champions—my parents, my dad's identical twin who treated me like another daughter, his father-in-law who sang a special song only to me, my younger brother who worshipped the ground I walked on (even with all my relentless teasing), and my best friend who always sang my praises. But even they couldn't restructure how I viewed my adopted self. Not biological. Second best.

My parents did their best to raise me. I was their child. I was nurtured. I was white, growing up in a white family. I blended in well enough. But they couldn't erase my adoption. They couldn't provide a remedy for the one condition that made me different from them in almost every way—nature.

I became good at skipping around the probing questions that were impossible to answer, questions that always left me wondering.

Why was I given away?

Who are my birth parents? What do they look like? What do they do? Do they miss me?

Where do I come from?

FOUR

Keeping my mind busy became impossible as I waited to hear my test results. The hospital waiting room had its standard array of magazines, which I flipped through. Nervous, my fingers stuck to the slick pages. It was June 1997, and I had driven east across the country from Colorado to start a summer program on Nantucket, where I would earn the last few credits I needed to complete my Master's in Civil Engineering. I was on track to graduate that August and then, God willing, find a job with my newly minted degree. It was hard to think about the future with a looming, potentially deadly medical diagnosis.

One week earlier, I woke up to find a lump in my left breast—large and round, and it seemed to grow overnight. A friend who worked as a nurse in a large Boston hospital quickly got me an appointment with a well-known breast surgeon who appeared and waved me back. There were no smiles or pleasantries exchanged as we walked in silence down the long corridor to the examination room. The surgeon led me into a room with an incredible view of downtown Boston—a space reserved for a twenty-four-year-old woman who was about to be told that they needed their breast removed. The surgeon closed the door and clipped the scans completed an hour earlier on the wall x-ray viewer. Still studying the films, she asked, "Is there a family history of breast cancer?" I told her that I was adopted and didn't have any medical history. She snapped her head around and demanded to know why I didn't have that information. In a tone suited for scolding a naughty child, she said, "That information would be vital to have." I just stared at her in disbelief. I was angry—for her lack of compassion, for her poor bedside manner, but also because she was right. Why didn't I know my medical history?

I had become used to answering the family history section on medical intake forms with my standard "adopted – unknown." Until that moment in the breast surgeon's office, I considered it an annoyance more than anything, a reminder that I was different from most patients. But I learned that if I didn't answer the question, the doctor eventually asked. I had to admit to being adopted.

The surgeon turned back to the scans to examine them more. She wasn't sure what the mass was in my breast, but she knew it needed to come out immediately. The lump was fast-growing, and the surgeon wanted to have it biopsied. "If I knew your family history, we might be taking a different approach," she said while pulling the scans off the viewer, placing them in my growing file, and then walking out the door without saying another word. The white tissue paper that followed me as I jumped off the examination table broke the silence. After pealing the crinkly trail off my sticky legs, I left the room without looking back at the city skyline.

The procedure could not wait until the end of summer. I started my program on Nantucket Island and then flew back to Boston a couple of weeks later for surgery. I would later leave Nantucket with my last graduate credits and a two-inch scar across my breast.

My parents flew up from Florida to be with me during my surgery and recovery. We were all concerned about what the biopsy would reveal, but I didn't tell them about my conversation with the surgeon—that having my medical history was important. Instead of considering I might be the victim of some mysterious genetic abnormality, my mom became fixated on my caffeine intake and its possible effects. Once again, she placed the burden on me to alter my actions and behave perfectly. After waiting a week for the results, the mass was determined to be a non-cancerous growth. Genetics, not coffee, was likely to blame.

I bounced back quickly and finished up my program in early August. On my long drive back to Colorado, the clipped voice of my breast surgeon kept popping into my head. "Why don't you have any family medical information?" Good question. While I had recovered physically from the summer surgery, the experience left me emotionally drained. The surgeon's anxiety over the unknown fueled a latent desire to know so much more. Was there a family history of cancer? The surgeon's admonishment triggered my own angry response, the smoldering sense of injustice. I needed to muster up the courage to fight for my information.

I didn't know where to begin. Soon after my formal adoption in March 1973, my parent's contact with the adoption agency ended. Were post-adoption services available? I didn't know.

My first task was to ask my dad to look through his files for my adoption paperwork. I did not doubt that if there were some hidden clue, he would have it. He is a closet hoarder, saving all the family mementos from his purging partner, who threw out her own wedding dress. When I had my first child, he pulled my doll cradle down from the attic for her. My grandfather made it for me, and I was so touched he'd saved it. My daughter's eyes lit up with excitement until she saw the occupant living inside for more than twenty years without a bath—a dirty, plastic-faced doll with matted hair suited for a horror movie, not a little girl. I imagine he has many of these "treasures" squirreled away throughout his large Florida attic, languishing year after year in the extreme heat.

But the only files that my dad could find were the court documents he filed for my adoption in 1973, papers that included my adoptive identity. There was no revealing information, such as an accidental reference to a birth mother or a birth name mistakenly written on one of the pages.

With no leads to help, I began scouring the shelves of my university library for books on adoption searches. I quickly learned that each state had its own set of adoption laws. In 1997, only two states allowed adoptees unconditional access to their original birth record, and Florida was not one of them. Living in Colorado did not make it easy to figure out what I had to do to request my sealed records that resided in Florida.

I learned of a local adoption-triad support group meeting through a flyer that I saw stapled to an information board on campus. Searching adoptees made up most of the group when I attended, but I left the meeting feeling more alone and confused. Why couldn't I just ask the adoption agency for my records? The group was familiar with the legal challenges of the sealed record system, and their discussion revolved more around searching tips—where to look, who to ask, and how to game the system. I took notes and kept a journal of anything that could potentially be useful. After two months of figuring out my options, I decided the next step to finding information was to reach out to the adoption agency. Through the support group, I heard something called a non-identifying information report, a report that an adoptee was entitled to by law and included summary information about my birth history and family. The report wasn't supposed to reveal any identifying information about the birth parents. Still, some adoptees can extract enough birth information from the report to conduct successful searches. I felt hopeful.

My dad helped me track down the adoption agency because the name and location that appeared on my court records had changed. When I called the agency, I struggled to find the right words to start the conversation. What did I really want? Medical information? Family history? Birth parent names? What I really wanted to know was how I came to be. What is it that makes me, me?

When the receptionist picked up my call, I heard myself simply say, "Hello, my name is Katherine, and I was adopted through your agency in the 1970s. I am requesting information about my adoption." She politely took my information and told me that someone would be in touch. About a week later, I received a letter from an adoption service coordinator, Laurie. This piece of correspondence was my first contact with the adoption agency, and all I could feel was disappointment after reading the coordinator's two-page typed letter. Laurie said it is against Florida law F.S. 63.162 to disclose identifying information without a court order. She went on to tell me that non-identifying details could be shared legally but that she didn't know what information, if any, was in my files. It would take her a few weeks to search because many old records were on microfilm. For a small fee, I was now at the mercy of an agency.

Before the agency released any information, I was required to verify my identity by mailing a notarized affidavit, a certified copy of my birth certificate, and a completed *Acknowledgement of Person* form. It was ironic to think I needed to prove who I am to learn more about who I am. Florida's statute allowed Laurie, a stranger, to look through my personal information, but not me. I had no legal right to my own identity.

Laurie's letter also stated that I could have my adoption file marked, indicating I wanted to be notified if a birth parent or other family members wanted contact. This was an option that I had never heard about before. The adoption agency never reached out to my parents with this information, and given this, it was likely that my birth parents didn't know about the possibility of contact. Once my adoption was finalized, there was no ongoing communication between the adoption agency and my birth mother or my parents. There was no mechanism to facilitate long-term contact—records, including contact information, were closed and sealed. The agency's obligations to me ended in 1973 with my final adoption decree. After that, I was on my own.

I read the statute that Laurie noted in her letter many years later, only to realize that F.S. 63.162 didn't exist when I was adopted. There was no law explicitly preventing the disclosure of identifying information.

Frustrated but determined, I followed the coordinator's instructions and quickly sent in all the necessary paperwork. Two months later, my non-identifying information report arrived.

I was kicking the snow off my boots when I pulled the agency's letter out of the mailbox. I could tell by its weight that it was more than one page. *The agency had information to report!* I hurried through the front door and ran up the stairs to my second-floor apartment, leaving a trail of slush on the wood treads behind. I shared my pistachio-green shingled Victorian with another tenant whose first-floor apartment wrapped around the historic home's common hall. The noise from my boots was probably deafening, but I couldn't get to my apartment fast enough, and being a considerate neighbor was the furthest thing from my mind. *What would the letter reveal?*

Once inside, I dropped my bag at the front door and opened the letter. The letter was my first glimpse of family history and the mystery of how I came to be. I was twenty-five.

> *Dear Katherine:*
>
> *Enclosed you will find your completed research and report of non-identifying information available to you from our records. The information was quite difficult to decipher, however, I am pleased to say that there was a good amount of information to report.*

I didn't read past the first paragraph of Laurie's cover page before quickly discarding it to reveal the report hiding underneath where my eyes settled on one line. *Your birth mother, Katherine…*

I was never good at being a Katherine as hard as I tried. Growing up with the nine-letter name was draining. It's a name that most people are too lazy to use in its entirety, even though its three syllables can easily be said in two. *Do you have a nickname I can use?* People always insisted on shortening Katherine, the most common being Kathy—a name I came to despise. Thankfully my parents had the foresight to give me the nickname Kacie, but it usually took a few roll calls at the beginning of each school year for the name to stick. *Katherine, Kathy, Kate, oh sorry, I mean Kacie.* Even my name struggles with identity.

I was named after my maternal great-grandmother, who passed away before I got a chance to remember her. She was born in Poland and immigrated as an adult. She never learned to speak English, and my mom never learned Polish, making me wonder how my mom communicated with her grandmother growing up. She said that the Polish language was her family's secret weapon to conceal conversations not meant to be overheard by her or her younger sister. When I was a baby, my mom took me on a trip to Ohio to meet my namesake for the first time. I have a photo of us sitting in a rocking chair, her cradling me in her arms while I stared wide-eyed at the person behind the camera, capturing the moment.

I finally grew into my name after college, determined to shed the immature name of Kacie for its more professional counterpart Katherine, but it doesn't always grab hold. Sometimes I am Katherine. Sometimes I am Kacie. I have even acquired the name Kate from my soccer mates, where everyone's name gets shortened to one syllable on the field. My name changes depending on the situation—fitting, I suppose, for an adopted girl.

What are the chances? It was a complete coincidence that my birth mother and I shared the name Katherine. As I stared down at the report, I thought about the moment when the social worker learned that my parents were going to name me Katherine. I imagined Charlotte sitting behind her desk at the adoption agency, facing my parents on the other side, willing her forehead and eyes not to reveal her surprise.

My entire birth history filled two-and-a-half typed pages. As I started to read, I tried to squash feeling cheated. My adoptive family's paternal lineage could fill an entire book with names dating to the 1300s. But Laurie had warned me that many old adoption records contain little or no information. I was one of the lucky adoptees to get a good amount of it at almost three pages. Shouldn't I feel grateful?

Along with learning the city and hospital of my birth, the report provided details about my birth family. There was a little bit of information about birth parent relatives, and learning about their physical attributes and interests was interesting. But what most captivated me were the details about my birth parents. The report dedicated an entire page to my birth mother, describing her physical attributes, ethnic background, and interests. I learned that she was an attractive, friendly, outgoing, and thoughtful young woman. I also learned that she was an honor roll student who planned to attend junior college the fall after my birth. The report went on to talk about the circumstances of my relinquishment.

> *She had been in a relationship with the birth father for a brief period of time. Shortly after she informed him of her pregnancy, their relationship ended. Neither felt they were ready for marriage or parenthood. The birth mother was able to discuss her position with her parents and inform them of her plans. She received their support and understanding. Several of her relatives and some of her very close friends knew of her pregnancy, however,*

she still felt it would be best for her to leave the area temporarily. She traveled from her home in Middlesex County, Massachusetts, to Florida to temporarily reside with friends of the family to arrange for adoption plans.

Katherine had to carry the burden of pregnancy by herself, a reality that made me sad even as I noted the positive spin woven by Laurie's words. My roots didn't begin in Florida as I had always believed, but near Boston. My birth mother traveled 1,300 miles to have her baby in secret. I later learned that Katherine's story was not unusual. Like so many single women of this post-war era, being sent away to have a baby was common. Some lived with family or friends, and some lived in maternity homes. In her book *The Girls Who Went Away,* Ann Fessler illustrates the double standard single pregnant women faced and how many of these women felt pressured or even coerced into relinquishing their children.[12]

The last paragraph of the maternal summary gave me some relief. It left me with the impression that adoption was her choice. She may have felt like she needed to leave her hometown to spare her family any embarrassment of her pregnancy, but in the end, she felt that adoption was in my best interest. I imagined that she felt comforted hearing more about the people I would come to know as mom and dad.

At some point during her pregnancy, she had the opportunity to meet with adoptive mothers. She felt this had been an extremely valuable experience, as it reassured her and supported her decision about adoption, feeling that it was in the best interest of her child. Some limited information was shared with her about the adoptive family, and she was very pleased with what she heard.

Paternal information was saved for the last page of my report. My birth father's generous sperm donation earned him a three-paragraph spread. Francis got 123 words. I quickly discovered that he was tall and lean with black hair, brown eyes, and a dark complexion, that he lived in Essex County, Massachusetts, was a high school graduate, worked as a mechanic, and played basketball. But it was the last paragraph of his section that left the most significant impression.

The birth mother informed the birth father of her pregnancy. He informed her that he did not feel as if he could help her in any way, and he terminated the relationship between them.

My birth father had no accountability and could simply walk away. I wondered why the agency decided to include that information. Honesty? To garner sympathy for a woman forced to go through a traumatic experience alone? I put myself in his young male shoes and wondered if I would have done the same thing.

I read and reread the report five times before leaving my front hall. I tried to form an image of the two people who created me from a few paragraphs, but it was hard. No one ever claimed me to be a child with an imagination—my long-legged doll was named "Longlegs" and my now dirty-faced, matted hair doll, "Baby." I didn't grow up with a vision of my birth parents. I didn't fantasize about them being doctors or famous actors. They were always a blank slate. But when I read through the report, I latched on to a few key points. In addition to sharing the same name as my birth mother, I inherited her curly hair and fair complexion. My height fell squarely in the middle of my two birth parents at 5'6". I was graced with my birth father's thinner frame and his mechanical and athletic abilities, although my game was soccer, not basketball.

I wondered if my mom had been given this birth family information in advance if she would have agreed to the adoption. Would she have been comforted by the details she heard as my birth mother had, or would she have chosen to take a hard pass? Given my birth parent's physical descriptions, I was unlikely to be gifted the traits she coveted: blond hair and blue eyes. My birth father was not college-educated with no apparent plans to attend. At 5'1" and 145 pounds, my birth mother was on the heavier side. Maybe this is what the social worker was trying to protect me from—preformed opinions before my parents had a chance to love me for me.

FIVE

The birth mother felt she had very little to offer her child, besides her love, and expressed feeling as if it would not be sufficient enough. She did not want to consider having her mother raise her child and was quite adamant about it. She had a lot of feelings for the baby and admitted it was an extremely painful experience for her, but nevertheless, felt she was doing the right thing. She wanted her baby to have every possible advantage and opportunity in life.

I tried to read between the lines, combing for hints to everything not disclosed. I picked it apart. The report confirmed that my birth mother was eighteen and single, facts that my parents always knew. What I didn't realize was that she was both a high school graduate and employed full-time when she became pregnant with me. Did she not want to be saddled with a baby as a single parent, or was there something more? Was someone concerned about my safety?

My dad may have told me this story out of guilt, how he almost got me killed. It was one of those tales where he cast himself as the hero and not the neglectful father. It was one of a handful of stories that I heard that made me wonder how I reached adolescence in one piece. I could hardly blame my parents. I was a very active and curious child. As soon as I could walk, which was very early at eight months, I was off exploring my world. I ran, climbed, and attempted to walk through walls. My parent's breaks came at night when I slept hard and in thirteen-hour clips building my reserves for the next day.

After my fourth trip to the hospital for stitches, a social worker questioned my parents for possible abuse. "We literally can't take our eyes off of her for one second," was their response. But that's exactly what happened and how I ended up at the bottom of a neighbor's pool.

I imagined my dad and me out on our evening bike ride—him on his black steel Schwinn knock-off and me perched behind in my green and black plaid child seat. He would be approached by a neighbor as we rode by who asked him about a pool pump issue. We had a pool, and my dad was an engineer, making him an expert. He would park his bike in the neighbor's driveway and lift me out of my seat. We would walk hand-in-hand to the side of the house, through the fence, and to the defective pump.

My dad would drop my hand as he took a closer look to find the problem. I would be distracted by a floating duck in the distance. I would quietly wander off to the pool's edge and try to grab the duck, but it would be just past my reach. I would lose my balance and fall. Consumed by water, I would sink. Realizing that he had dropped my hand, my dad would look around for me. Panic would set in when he no longer had me in his sights. He would run over to the pool and see a shadowy figure at the bottom, and he would jump in.

My dad saved me. This accident could happen to any parent, and it made me wonder what it was about my birth mother that deemed her unfit to raise me. Her age? My dad was in his early thirties at my near death. Her single status? My dad was solely in charge when I almost drowned.

The report also confirmed the known fact of a family history of diabetes but also mentioned a history of varicose veins, heart disease, and cancer. I thought back to when my parents told me about diabetes and if they had just forgotten about the other disclosed medical issues. When my dad could only produce court documents, I realized that my parents never wrote down anything the adoption agency told them about my birth history. Whatever they knew had been committed to memory.

My non-identifying information report seemed packed with information, yet it didn't feel like enough to answer all my questions. When I finally went back to read the cover page that Laurie included with the report, I found myself screaming at her in my mind. She concluded her letter by saying, "If you have any questions, please feel free to contact me." *Yes, Laurie! I have a lot of questions! What you provided is just a tiny snapshot of one period in time. How can I capture the essence of someone from your few written words? I am even more curious. I want to know more!*

The same day I received the report in the mail, I called my parents to tell them my exciting news. I had only discussed my desire to reach out to the adoption agency with my dad up until this point because I knew my mom wasn't too excited about my search. The adoption agency sold her on the idea that if she loved me enough, she would be enough. She never understood that it had nothing to do with her. I wasn't looking for a different mom or a replacement family. She was a fine mom, and I was blessed with a great family. But my love for my family and my desire for information are not mutually exclusive. Out there were two people who each gave me their DNA. My family and my DNA are both a part of me.

My mom and I were close until we weren't. I don't recall that exact moment when the shift in our relationship occurred, but the teenage years must have been hard for her. Before then, she had been able to exert some level of control. Maybe she found it easier to relate to a child so different from her if she could control just one element that made us more alike—something like clothes. As an artist, she dressed in high fashion. Seeing her kids as an extension of her, we were always impeccably dressed, either in clothes she made herself, or something picked off the boutique rack. As my brothers and I grew into adolescence, we developed our own tastes. My mom seemed to have an easier time letting go of control over my brothers, maybe because they were boys. Or perhaps because it was easier for her to focus on one child and, as the only girl, I drew the short straw. I began to fight her on everything—

clothes, friends, boyfriends, and even curfew when my older brother got to stay out later than me. I preferred navy blue to pink and soccer shorts to dresses. Although I knew she loved and supported me, there was always a low-level tension between us. I avoided discussing anything emotional or controversial, and as a busy teenager, it became easier to avoid each other most days.

When I was out of the house, my dad pleaded with me to change how I interacted with my mom. "You have to meet her where she is," he told me. "She endured a lot of trauma as a child," he went on. Her life was traumatic growing up poor in a large midwestern city where her dad struggled to hold a job. It was just one of many hardships. But for me to change felt like a huge ask from my dad, thinking, *Didn't I experience trauma too*? But I did change. I adapted my behavior, and my relationship with my mom improved. It took me some time to realize why my dad asked such a colossal favor of his daughter—I could adapt, pivot, and even change. Being adopted helped me hone these skills, and I got quite good.

Even so, I always tiptoed around the adoption and birth family subjects to spare my mom's feelings. But when she was the one to pick up the phone when I called, I found myself blurting out, "I have the same name as my birth mother!" before catching myself. She handed the phone over to my dad, and I knew the conversation was over before it started. My dad said he would call me right back, but the call didn't come until the next day when my mom was out of the house. He was excited for me. He once told me that he would support me if I ever decided to search for my birth parents. He even paid the $85 fee required to get my non-identifying report. I know that he still supported me even though he told me he couldn't talk about my birth family. He didn't want to upset my mom. I tried to understand. They wanted me to remain their child, and my mom wanted me to be the child whose past only included them. My desire to find my birth mother must mean that something is wrong with the mother assigned to me. My mom wanted to be the perfect mom. She wanted to be the hero too.

My mom wanted to keep her kids close, yet she pushed all of us out of Florida. After putting so much effort into building a family, it was hard to understand why she wanted our unit disbanded once we were adults. She hated Florida. She felt forced to live there because of my dad's career. And because she hated the State, us remaining there meant she failed as a parent. But Florida was the only home I'd ever known, and it was hard for me to think about leaving it behind. I struggled to commit to a college during my senior year of high school, and when I finally settled on a Florida university, I sensed my mom's disappointment. She encouraged me to start that summer, giving me time to change my mind and transfer to one of her out-of-state choices that fall. But I had fun that summer semester, registered for fall classes, and moved from my summer dorm to an off-campus apartment with my best friend from high school.

And then the murders began.

We didn't hear about university students being killed inside their apartments until halfway through our first week of fall classes. By then, five people were dead. The first two bodies found were young women, incoming freshmen who lived a mile away along the same stretch of road. The crime scene was the stuff of horror movies—rape, torture, mutilation. The killer entered the apartment at night while the women were sleeping. It could easily have been us. We fit the profile in every way, from what we looked like to where we lived. It was a scary time, but I don't remember being scared. My roommate and I had already survived a school shooting two years earlier during a time when assault-style weapons were hard to get, and causalities were limited to what a handgun could inflict. Three people were shot, one died. That experience hardened me. I learned to live in a world where bad things happened.

The university canceled classes for a week, and my dad picked me up to visit another college in Alabama, where I was already accepted. I was one of many students who transferred out that fall. Enduring a school shooting and the terror of the Gainesville Ripper, as the murderer was later called, felt like a sign that I needed to move on and out of Florida. Maybe my mom was right.

It was now the security of the 2,000 miles between us that shielded me from the disappointment that their faces undoubtedly revealed on the other end of the phone. It was one thing to hear that they were not interested in my birth history and another to see the displeasure written all over their faces. I expected my parents to be happy for me, not threatened by my discoveries, and my excitement deflated after the exchange with them. We had grown used to the weekly phone calls, getting caught up on nothing serious. I caught them off guard, and they weren't ready for what I had to say. I should have waited until we could all sit down together in the same room. I should have prepped them. For the first time in my life, I moved forward without their support.

For the next six months, I immersed myself in finding a job. I never lost sight of continuing my adoption search journey, but it became an arduous task to attempt any search effort from the other side of the country. My life began in Boston. I lived in Colorado. Other things became more pressing—like starting a professional career to help pay for the bills that had been slowly piling up since graduation.

That summer, I landed a dream job that brought me to the east coast and within six hours of where my story likely began. When I looked out over the city skyline listening to my breast surgeon quiz me about my unknown family medical history, I had no idea that I would be returning one year later looking for those answers. Boston, I thought, was the place where all the clues to my past were hidden. I needed to make a slight detour and start there.

It is a story my dad loves to tell—how I swindled him out of his car, twice. It is a story I hate hearing—it makes me sound like a spoiled child (which I absolutely was). But my dad can always spin this particular tale in a way that makes him look like the gullible pushover—indulging his only daughter by never being able to say no, proof of his love. He always got to be the hero.

When my sixteenth birthday rolled around and I got my driver's license, my parents assumed that I would drive the old family wagon—something resembling the green Griswold family truckster after reaching Wally World with its faux wood paneling now peeling away from its steel backing and a grille that looked like it was missing a couple of teeth. With my older brother now off to college, it was ready to be passed down to me.

For two and a half years, my brother tested the limits of the wagon. He drove it through a car wash with its windows open—probably the only time the green vinyl seats got a proper cleaning. He proved that the wagon could not go the 120 miles per hour predicted by the dashboard speedometer—he got it just past 100 miles per hour before the wagon shook violently in protest (that may have been when one of the hubcaps mysteriously went missing). Under my brother's custody, it was dubbed "the urban assault vehicle" by his friends, and the wagon earned several feature spots on the high school's video broadcast channel. But what would a teenage girl growing up in the 1980s do with a beat-up old station wagon? How could I possibly transform it into a cool status symbol as my brother had done?

The station wagon sat idle, backed up in the driveway, looking like it'd rather be lawn furniture than a vehicle. At ten years old, it had given up. It lost its ability to go in reverse, needing a good ten-minute warm-up before it even considered moving in any direction but forward. It made sense that my dad didn't give a second thought to the impacts of being provided a car with no ability to back up. Reverse, in his mind, was a luxury. For an entire year, he drove a car after a bad accident that left two huge dents on the driver's side. He never complained about entering the car from the passenger side door and sliding across the bench seat to the other side with the steering wheel. He had to lean a little to the left to drive the car, but he never worried much about the fine details. He was someone who spent ten hours fixing something if it meant saving $10. He enjoyed the challenge. He later rebuilt the wagon's compressor to fit in the glovebox when the air conditioning gave out. His handiwork made the glovebox unusable and dangerously hot. When the dashboard started to show signs of melting, he resorted to switching the air conditioning on and off as needed. My dad always found the affordable workaround.

He tried to alleviate my worry, "Just back into the parking space when you get to school." He made it sound so easy. But I had hardly grasped the concept of backing up. Turning my head, looking behind, and navigating something as long as a yacht into a slot that seemed more fitting of a matchbox car was not easy. And that was when the first swindle occurred. He sensed my growing anxiety, resigned to my demands for a better car, and handed over the keys to his. He drove the wagon, and I drove his smaller, less conspicuous manual coupe with the optional gas gauge. It was easier for me to figure out how many miles I could go before the car needed refueling than to learn how to back up, one more symptom of my forward-moving conditioning.

Now I was packing up my life in Colorado into the second swindle—the black Saab he'd bought used and drove for three months before I convinced him I needed a better car for my long drive west to graduate school. This car, I told him, was everything I needed for the snowy climate that I would endure. The Saab was perfect. It could move forward and back, taking me to new adventures, to a new life, and to my story's beginning—to the place where I began.

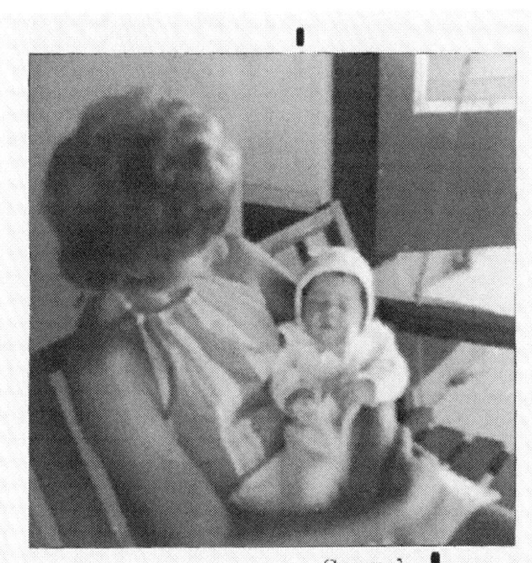

Search

SEARCH

August 1972, Father

They had been waiting two years to adopt a baby girl when Joyce woke up in a panic. Out of breath by the time she found him sitting in the family room reading the morning newspaper, she pulled the paper out of his hands and said emphatically, "No, we are going to wait for the girl." And as quickly as she came into the room, she left, dropping the newspaper in his lap without saying another word.

Richard picked up the ringing phone the evening before. Charlotte's voice was chipper when she'd said, "We have a baby boy that will be ready to go home tomorrow afternoon." A baby boy, a healthy newborn relinquished by his birth mother a day earlier, was ready to adopt. The process to adopt Jeff four years before had only taken nine months, and he could tell that Joyce was getting anxious from the long wait. *Might she consider adopting another boy?* He wondered and told Charlotte that he would discuss it with his wife and call her back.

He took a long, deep breath after placing the receiver back in its cradle. They already had one son, and Joyce was hoping to add a baby girl to their family. He didn't really have an opinion one way or another. After years of fertility problems, he just wanted to see his wife happy.

He found Joyce in the upstairs nursery reading a book in the rocking chair. This routine had become her nightly ritual after tucking Jeff in for the night. They'd moved Jeff to a new room about a year earlier to redecorate the nursery for a girl and make room for her arrival. The furniture was the same. The vertical striped, white-blue-olive wallpaper remained on three of the four walls. But she changed the blue wall to olive and painted large colorful flowers. She was a talented artist who had an eye for design. He was impressed that she was able to reuse 75% of the room's contents and still make it look like a completely new room.

He poked his head in and said, "Charlotte just called." He saw her face light up with excitement. "She said that they have a baby available now if we would consider adopting a boy." The glow in her eyes started to fade, and she sat there for a minute without saying anything. He knew that trying to talk his wife into something was futile. He let the silence sit between them. Her gaze shifted from him to the olive-green wall. He stood in the doorway and watched as her head moved from one of the painted flowers to the blue butterfly above. It was the only butterfly she'd painted in the sea of flowers, and it looked as if it were flying out of the room.

Without taking her eyes off the butterfly, she finally said, "Okay."

There wasn't much more discussion between them. He went downstairs and called Charlotte. "Joyce and I have decided to adopt the baby boy."

He heard Charlotte say, "Great," before going on to tell him that she'd call back in the morning with more details. But the next day, before Charlotte had even had the chance, he called to say they'd had a change of heart. After sleeping on it overnight, he and Joyce agreed that they would wait for their baby girl.

September 1972, Mother

In her heart of hearts, she'd known a girl would come to her to raise. Only a few days after declining Charlotte's offer to adopt a baby boy, the social worker called to say that there was a baby girl available. "The baby can come home today," she heard Charlotte say.

"Yes!" she said without hesitation. "Yes, we want this baby girl."

When the phone rang, she and Jeff were finishing breakfast. Jeff had run off to play while she was on the phone, and she found him under the stairs, in his hideout, with his red wicker toy box. "Jeff," she said, "your baby sister is coming home today. Daddy is on his way home, and we are going to meet her." He had been excited about becoming a big brother, and he immediately got to his feet and started jumping with excitement. She could hear the sticking sound of his vinyl-footed pajamas on the slate floor.

She had been ready for this day for a long time but found herself staring into the closet, trying to figure out what to wear. She'd already dressed Jeff in her favorite orange and blue plaid jumper and packed the outfit she'd chosen for the baby nearly a year ago. Now she was struggling to select the perfect outfit to meet her daughter, her mind wandering to the first moment she would hold her little girl. She finally settled on a bright, sleeveless mini dress she'd bought earlier that summer, practical only for its fashion and the hot, humid weather.

She was packing up the diaper bag when Richard walked through the door. They had another hour before they had to leave, and she knew that he would spend every second of that time documenting the moment. Putting his brief-case down on the kitchen peninsula and loosen-loosening his tie, he set off to grab his Super 8 video camera. He shot footage of her and Jeff on the living room couch, standing next to the bassinet, and walking out the door with the diaper bag, Jeff following behind. She would appreciate having this video later because all she could focus on at that moment was her new baby girl. What would she look like? Would she have blonde hair like her? Would she have blue eyes like Jeff? Would she grow up to be an engineer like her dad? She had been waiting for so long. She couldn't wait to meet Katherine.

February 1973, Richard

He was the eternal optimist, knowing that the proceeding was just a formality. But understanding this did little to calm his wife. She paced all night, going from their bed to Kacie's room and back before beginning the cycle again. He knew what was on Joyce's mind, that with the swift slam of the gavel, they could somehow be deemed unfit to be parents and have to leave their little girl behind. They had gone through this process once before with Jeff, so he couldn't quite understand why his wife was so unsettled. There was a mandatory six-month waiting period from the date of Kacie's birth before the court would hear their case and make the adoption official. Today's court appearance marked six months to the day. Charlotte hadn't had any concerns—she had already submitted her report to the court recommending that the adoption proceed. She deemed them fit to be parents. And yet, Joyce's nerves would not ease.

Her pacing did not end with breakfast or with the morning chaos that life with a baby and an almost four-year-old brings. He could swear there was now a wear mark in the living room shag carpet. She continued walking the same path as she got ready for their morning court date, holding Kacie tight and putting her down only long enough to get herself dressed.

Now sitting on the bench outside the judge's chambers, he could feel his wife's white-knuckle grip as they held hands. It had taken him a full five minutes to convince her to pass Kacie off to his mom, who had accompanied them to court and sat waiting with them. "We can't bring her in with us," he'd said soothingly. "I promise, she will still be right here when we get back."

When the court bailiff finally called them in, he felt the resistance in her hand as he stood up. "I promise," he said again. Joyce stood up and followed him through the door before taking one last look back at Kacie.

"Are you here on the adoption?" The judge was sitting on the other side of a large table, motioning for them to step in.

"Yes, sir," he replied.

"You all can just have a seat there," the judge said and pointed to two chairs opposite his seat. "This is kind of an informal proceeding." The judge swore them in and then asked to see the adoption petition he had prepared in advance. After sliding the paperwork across the table, they waited in silence for the judge to respond.

"Rather than have you present the testimony here, if you don't mind, I will just ask you questions and move things along a little faster." The judge began with him, asking questions about when he and Joyce were married, his occupation, their home life, and how the child was doing. *Easy enough*, he thought and looked over at his wife to give her a reassuring smile.

"How old is the child you seek to adopt?" the judge asked.

"Six weeks." He knew as soon as he said it, it was wrong.

Before he could correct himself, he felt a slight nudge to the ribs from under the table and heard Joyce say, "She is six months."

"Just a minute," the judge interrupted, "let your husband speak, and you listen to what he says, and I will ask you to confirm it." The judge waited for Joyce to nod in the affirmative before going on.

He got hung up on one other question from the judge, this time about his son's age. His response of, "He will be four months in April" was met with another, harder nudge from his wife.

"Four years in April," she said. When the judge turned to Joyce, she said, "I'll be quiet," before he had the chance to give her another warning for speaking out of turn.

The rest of the proceedings went as he expected. The judge allowed Joyce to answer her own set of questions and correct his testimony. He thought he saw the flash of a slight smile emerge on the judge's face when she said, "The boy is four years old, and the girl will be six months old tomorrow."

February 1973, Joyce

With the judge's final recommendation for adoption in hand, she couldn't get out of the courtroom fast enough. What a dope, she left thinking. How could Richard not correctly answer the simple question of their children's ages? Deep down, she knew these misstatements wouldn't prevent the adoption. She knew he was nervous, too, despite his steely façade. As she stepped out of the courthouse and into the cool February breeze clutching her daughter tight, she could hear her husband whisper the word, "Breathe." She heard Richard take one long deep breath with her when she did.

SIX

I have this recurring dream. In it, I am standing in a stark white room next to a bright, lemon-colored rotary dial desk phone. At least, I think it's me. I see my hand as it reaches out to make a call. I see my curls fall next to my face as I bend over to dial—one curl wound so tight it is hard to see where it ends and the phone cord begins as I pull the handset to my face. I see my long index finger insert itself into the plastic dial to call someone. *Swish. Dah, dah, dah, dah, dah.* Again. *Swish. Dah, dah, dah.* And again.

The girl in my dream makes it to the last number before she realizes she's misdialed. She pushes the plastic button in the handset cradle down and releases it. She starts again. *Swish. Dah, dah, dah, dah, dah.* She makes it all the way to the last digit and another misdial. She tries again. Misdial. And again. *Swish. Dah, dah, dah, dah, dah.*

After the fourth misdial, the girl gives up. She slams the handset back down into its cradle in frustration. The phone gives a quick *brr-ring* from the force as if willing her to keep trying. *You will get the number right this time.*

The long drive east gave me too much time to think. *The Boston metropolitan region is enormous! Where do I even begin?* I picked up a map of the Boston area before leaving Colorado and studied it during my first overnight stop. Somewhere in Iowa, I pulled off the interstate to a cheap motel just beyond the town's only stoplight. With the map spread across one of the room's double beds, I could visualize the expanse of the two counties situated north of Boston, Middlesex County and Essex County—the last reported areas where my birth parents lived. *Why couldn't they be from a small town?* I imagined walking from my motel room to the diner across the street and someone recognizing me. Everyone knows everyone in a small town. "Hey, do you know so-and-so? You look so much like her. She lives right around the corner near such-and-such," someone would say as I ate fries. Mystery solved.

Being from a large city started to make my search feel daunting. I figured the logical place to start was with my birth mother. The adoption agency gave her the most amount of real estate in my non-identifying information report, and likely she would be the easiest person to find. But I also felt she was the person I needed to find first. She carried me, and she'd be the one to give me up nine months later.

I sat down on the bed opposite the map to reread my report and jotted down key facts. I was born in a military hospital in Florida. My birth mother lived in Massachusetts. She had curly auburn hair, brown eyes, and a reported ethnicity of German and Irish. She worked for the telephone company.

Male first names were not provided. Coincidence? Trickery? Searching based on female names alone would be difficult because they could assume married names.

When was it written? There was no date. The birth mother's stated age was eighteen. Was that at agency intake or when she gave birth? It could mean as much as a six-month difference, and that could make determining her exact birth year challenging. Finding her felt near impossible without a full name and birthdate, or even a birth year. So, I focused on the one date that the agency documented, that she was to attend junior college in September 1972. I decided to start there.

I took a break from two long days of driving east to see my grandma. Her home, and now my home for the next few days, was a place I'd spend part of my summer as a child exploring the mountains I loved and experiencing small-town life with friends I developed over the years.

My grandma and I were close, as close as anyone with five decades and two generations separating them could be. If I had to pick anyone I was most like in my family, it would be her. If you studied our faces enough, you could probably see some resemblance. But it was more the way she lived her life that most resembled mine. She was tough as nails and not the typical female of her generation. She was an only child, and there were no limits put on her as to what she could or couldn't do with her life. She attended business school and was working when she met my grandfather, who arrived in her small town from New York to open a corner store. Once they were married, they ran the business together—him the store and her the books. They became successful enough to move across town and build the area's first modern-day grocery from the ground up.

My grandma was from Driftwood, a name that sums up the town with its small scattering of buildings cast along a river east of the Allegheny Mountains. Her great-grandfather built the family's Gothic Revival homestead in 1874, shortly after immigrating from Ireland. Born in 1916 in its second-floor back bedroom, she weighed only one pound according to family lore—her body and limbs were so tiny that her dad could slip his wedding band up to her shoulder. Her sister, born one year later, also a preemie, didn't survive past her first two weeks of life. My grandma lived to be ninety-four.

With its ornate details and large parlor, the house served as the family gathering spot for many occasions, including births and deaths. In her early teens, my grandma moved away. Her uncle went on to live in the house until 1963, when he died, and the family sold the house.

The house slowly fell into disrepair until it was purchased in 2001 by a couple committed to its restoration. Reportedly haunted, a fact described by my family who lived there, the new owners were eager to tell me all about the handful of unexplained events when I visited the homestead for the first time in 2003. Nothing sinister, they assured me—simply waking up to the smell of bacon when no one was in the kitchen cooking or a helping hand lightening the load on an otherwise heavy beam the owners were attempting to muscle in place during foundation stabilization work.

When I asked to use the bathroom before leaving, they commented how the house would know an ancestor had come back to visit. The only bathroom was a converted upstairs bedroom claimed when a prior family installed indoor plumbing years earlier. With the outhouse long gone, the owners located the backfilled pit and were excavating it for its hidden treasures. The outhouse served not only as a dumping ground for human waste but also as the family trash bin. During my house tour, the owners proudly pointed out their bookcase display of unearthed glass vials they'd cleaned to showcase their beautiful blue-green color. I imagined the contents they once held—a myriad of elixirs that have probably since been deemed unsafe for consumption.

The second floor was not part of the tour, and my guides left me at the bottom of the stairs to find the bathroom. I slowly wandered up the steep winder absorbing all the detail, and wondered if I would get the chance to meet a past family spirit. I knew who they all were, having studied our Irish side of the family tree in preparation for my trip. Apart from the new plumbing fixtures, not much had changed upstairs. The house felt haunted with its Victorian-era wallpaper peeling off the walls and bare patches of lath where the plaster had loosened its grip. But there was no mysterious creak of the floorboard or faint breeze that made the hairs on the back of my neck stand on end during my visit. I couldn't blame the spirits for not showing themselves to their kin. I don't share the same blood that once ran through their veins. How could they know we were related?

I pulled into the single-lane driveway that ran the entire length of my grandmother's house—just far enough off the brick street to clear the sidewalk and the telephone pole my mom managed to back into three decades earlier while visiting my dad during a college break. My black Saab hatchback, with its green Colorado license plate and bright yellow, roof-mounted bike rack, stuck out amongst the neighbor's American-made counterparts. When I was in town the next afternoon buying some groceries, someone approached me and said, "Hey, you must be Peg's visitor from Colorado." I smiled and nodded, thinking back to Iowa. Everyone knew my grandma Peg and now everyone apparently knew she had a visitor from Colorado. *It is hard to stay hidden in a small town.*

Once I arrived in Boston, I asked my local contact about junior colleges in the area and decided to visit a community college near an air force base. The college was around in 1972, and my report indicated that my birth mother's father was retired from the Air Force. Maybe my birth mother's family settled near the base.

One search technique I picked up at the adoption triad

support group was looking through old high school yearbooks. When I scanned the map back in Iowa and saw the number of high schools that probably existed in Middlesex County (population 1.5 million), visiting junior colleges first made more sense—until I started looking through those yearbooks. "So, you are not a student or an alumnus? Why do you want to look through old yearbooks?" the librarian asked. I perceived her tone as more accusatory than curious until she pointed out where the books were kept. The entire college collection of yearbooks filled one library shelf, their thin spines ordered by year. When I started flipping through 1972 and 1973's books, I realized that the librarian probably never received a request like mine. There was nothing to them or in them. I expected to find ordered photos of students that attended, wearing their best outfits and flashing their biggest smiles. But the books only consisted of collages of people with no names attached. I had picked one of the more prominent junior colleges to begin my search, and it was here that I abandoned this route with no backup plan to pursue. I came back to my friend's house feeling defeated. It was day one.

My contact learned about an adoption search organization located in Essex County. Someone she knew had success finding his birth mother through the organization. She encouraged me to reach out to her friend. When he told me about the fee, hiring help seemed impossible for someone who hadn't even earned their first professional paycheck. It seemed like a logical avenue to pursue, but the option was out of my reach.

I spent the remainder of my time in Boston charting my next move and driving through the smaller towns of Middlesex County, where maybe someone would take notice of the stranger who looked like their friend so-and-so around the corner. I left two weeks later, having gotten no closer to finding any answers. My Saab left Boston in defiance, making it just over the George Washington Bridge before dying. *Stop spinning our wheels.* A tow truck took us the rest of the way.

SEVEN

Here is what I think I know.

I was born to a young, unwed woman named Katherine who gave me away because ~~I wasn't good enough.~~ she wanted her baby to have every possible advantage and opportunity in life.

It is against Florida Statute 63.162 to disclose identifying information about my birth parents.

I am German, Irish, French, and English.

Francis, my birth father, sounds like a douche.

August 1998

My hair was being unreasonable. I'd had it chopped into a pixie cut, thinking I'd finally be able to take advantage of a fashion trend in my low humidity locale. But when I was offered a job in the mid-Atlantic, I knew I had made a mistake. I grew up thinking I had big hair. In Florida, I was a walking hygrometer. *It is going to be hot and sticky today,* I'd see my hair say. Who needed a weather forecast? When I moved to Colorado, I realized that my hair's bigness came from its curls—tight curls that lost all excitement out west, where the dry climate allowed them to relax into large waves. Now I looked the part, a Jersey Girl in New Jersey, my hair reminiscent of an eighties style when my mom cut it almost to the scalp to remove the lice eggs that hitched a ride from school and refused to let go of my thick curls.

My new office was an open studio situated on the third floor of an old 1920s red brick building. Someone had placed an ancient air conditioning unit in one of its large, double-hung windows, but it managed only to provide a light, cool breeze and labored loudly to do that. I had done my best to trick my hair into thinking we were still out west, but the tight curls started to emerge even before I walked through the door for my first day of work. I was late and had already spent too much time out in the August air getting my broken car to a shop and securing a rental in its place. I had come to work in pants and a cardigan, and I was a sweaty mess. When I settled into my assigned desk, I noticed everyone else in shorts and sandals. I felt like I had arrived to climb a mountain wearing flip-flops. "It gets pretty hot up here," one of my new coworkers said after she'd looked me over. "You can pretty much wear what you want as long as you don't have client meetings." Her eyes settled on my hair after watching me attempt to press it down without success. "Don't worry. We have a lot of big hair up here!" Her eyes moved to the two other curly-haired women in the office.

My new studio space felt welcoming, and I instantly felt at ease with my coworkers. Our discussion of the third-floor environment led to me explaining why I was late for my first day of work. I had become more open to talking about my adoption because it was a hard topic to avoid. The search for my birth mother began to consume my life. I was excited, and it was all I could think and talk about. I was getting used to answering all the questions that usually followed. People seemed excited by my search, and I took the inquiries less personally.

After blaming and cursing my car, I went on to talk about why I took a sizeable detour through Boston. I hadn't even been formally introduced to everyone yet, and I was already spilling my guts. I looked around to see four sets of eyes staring at me intently, listening to everything I was saying. *Great. First I'm late, and now I'm responsible for the third floor's lack of productivity.*

When I finally finished, Big Hair with the thick Jersey accent said, "You mean you don't know who gave birth to you? That's fucking ridiculous!"

When I started my job, we had one computer on the first floor connected to the internet. Internet access was limited to slow dial-up modem connections, and doing internet research from New Jersey was still several years away. There were other tools, and one that my new coworker and insta-friend was now standing in front of my desk explaining to me. "LexisNexis is a people search engine." She went on to tell me about a friend of a friend who used it for work. I sent Friend-of-a-Friend what I knew, and she admitted that what she could provide was extremely limited without a last name. There were over 300 Katherines in Massachusetts. She narrowed her search to include different variations of the name Katherine who had some connection to Florida or were born between 1952 and 1955. I got ten, each name with a current address and phone number listed underneath.

I studied the names for days hoping that one would offer some secret clue—an Irish last name or an obvious tie to Florida. *Call me. I am your birth mother.* I thought about how I would open a phone conversation with someone who may, or more likely, may not be my birth mother. I thought about having to repeat that ten times. I was an amateur researcher with absolutely no idea what I was doing. I finally filed the list of names in my search journal for later, putting it out of my mind until years later.

June 2003

I met a guy. We got married. Life was happening, and my search stalled. I started thinking about searching for my birth mother again when I discovered that getting pregnant would be a challenge. Apparently, the fibrous growths that once inhabited my breast tissue were now taking up residence in my uterus. We didn't spend too much time discussing in-vitro fertilization or surrogacy as a path to parenthood before deciding to adopt. My husband and I had already discussed adoption as one way to build a family before we got married. It was vital that we were on the same page—that adoption was an option and not considered a second choice.

But when, a few years into marriage, we discovered our fertility issues, my heart sank. Not because we would turn to adoption, but because I wasn't sure how to cope with the reality of never having a genetic connection with anyone.

With some meager savings in the bank, I hired the small search organization my Boston contact told me about in 1998. The service included a professional search with the help of volunteers along with registration in local and national reunion registries. Of course, they couldn't guarantee a successful reunion but boasted a 99% success rate and an average search time of six to eight months. They assured me that even though Florida's records are closed to an adult adoptee, a proper search could bring about a successful reunion—all for a fee of $600.

In July 2004, the organization told me that their research team had been working with thirty-two possible last names for the previous year and ruled out over half. The passive reunion registry did not yield any results—no birth relatives were waiting to be contacted. The two scant research summaries I received since signing up with the organization and handing over my fee were brief and gave me no new information. They assured me that they were working hard on my case and would be in touch with any new developments. I was allowed to check in regarding the status of my search every six months, and I did until I gave up in 2007. News of finding my birth mother never came, and my phone calls and emails slowly went unanswered. I wondered how many cases were never solved and remained perpetually open. How did cases like mine fit into their near-perfect success rate?

October 2007

My best friend and I took a road trip to Boston. I had developed a search journal stuffed with information by now, and I decided to revisit my 1998 plan to look through old high school yearbooks. Because of the military connection, I assumed that my birth mother's family settled around Hanscom Air Force Base. I prioritized my search to the cities surrounding the base where most of the libraries kept copies of their local high school yearbooks. We scoured the books for any Katherines and name variations such as Katharine, Kathrine, Kathleen, Katie, Kate, Kathy, and even Kacie. I had some of my birth mother's siblings' names from my non-identifying information report. Still, we could not cross-reference any names or possible ages in later yearbooks. I diligently wrote down every name anyway and made photocopies of the pages with promising prospects. Who knew if all the information in my report was accurate? I didn't want to miss any clues.

One librarian suggested we also look through city directories for the year my birth mother lived in the area. These directories contain a list of residents along with their addresses and occupations. They are also in alphabetical order by last name. Without a last name, it felt like it would take years to scan through the thick books. I began to think the only real way to find my birth mother was to move to Boston or have my face put on a milk carton. Wasn't I a missing child too?

Unlike government officials, most librarians were willing to help because they had no duty to enforce adoption laws. I didn't feel like a criminal searching for my own identity with librarians.

Taking our long list of collected names, my friend and I spent a day at the Office of Vital Records in Dorchester. The office allowed genealogical research, but you had to come armed with specific names to research, and time was limited. Records were only available in person, and you couldn't leave the office with copies or photos. We produced a name, and the clerk brought a book bound with birth records turned to the name requested. The office instructed us to view only that specific record and return the book, but the temptation to quickly scan through the books for all Katherines born between 1953 and 1954 was too great. We didn't get too far before the clerk reminded us of the rules, but then she put her head back down, and we did it again. Our time eventually ran out before we got thrown out for our scandalous behavior, and we left with an even longer list of Katherines. Did you know that almost every variation of the name Katherine made the top sixty-five list of popular baby girl names for both 1953 and 1954? I didn't either.

April 2008

Feeling like I was running low on options, I hired a large professional search company that charged a hefty fee. This company utilized paid staff for their search efforts and promised to provide a report at the end of the search, either to document their success or their failure if, after one year, their searching proved futile—which it did. They could find nothing in historical or public records. There was no notice of adoption relinquishment naming a birth mother found in any local newspaper. Birth indexes listing birth information are not publicly available in Florida. My non-identifying report yielded no valuable information. The military hospital in which I was born disposed of all records that pre-dated 1999. And there was no evidence that any birth family members ever searched for me. A decade into my search, I learned that finding any record of my existence before my adoption was seemingly impossible.

I never fully understood why I was legally barred from my own information and why many states continue to keep adoption records under such a tight seal. All the non-adopted people in my life knew their birth parents' names and their genealogy. They had copies of their actual birth certificates. I had to take on the identities of the family in which I was placed and, I guess, just be grateful that I had been given life and a family. One of the most compelling cases I read in favor of opening sealed adoption records appeared in the *Journal of Constitutional Law* in 1999, which argued for a solution "that allows for change over time."[13] At the time of child relinquishment, it's the birth parents' and adoptive parents' identity and wishes that are most relevant. Once the child matures into adulthood, the adopted child's interests should begin to outweigh decisions made at the time of relinquishment because "openness may be much more central to her identity than continued secrecy is to the identities of the birth (or adoptive) parents."[14] Both sets of my parents may have wanted secrecy back in 1972, but was that still the case when I was twenty, thirty, or even forty? And what about my rights as an adult?

Florida enacted its first adoption legislation in 1885, and for six decades, the State did not seal adoption records or deem them confidential.[15] In 1939, Florida began to seal original birth certificates and issue amended birth certificates for adoptions but didn't restrict adoptees from accessing their original birth certificates until 1977.[16] The first substantial change in Florida's adoption law regarding confidentiality came in 1947 with an amendment that sealed court records and made all records confidential.[17] The intent behind sealing records was not designed to deny adoptees access but an attempt "to erase the stigma of illegitimacy by ensuring equal status and treatment of adopted and non-adopted offspring."[18]

When the court finalized my adoption in March 1973, it fell under the 1971 Florida Statute, which addressed confidentiality under Florida Statute 63.181.

> ***63.181 Adoption records confidential.*** *The court files, records and papers in the adoption of minors are confidential, and shall be indexed only in the name or names of the petitioners seeking the adoption and the name of the minor neither before nor after the adoption shall be noted on any docket, index or other record outside of the court file. At any time during the progress of the action the court may impound all files, records and papers therein. In all adoption actions on entry of a final judgement, the court files, records and papers shall be sealed and shall not be open to inspection except on order of the court. All adoption records of the division of family services of the department of health and rehabilitative services and licensed child-placing agencies are hereby declared to be confidential and shall not be open to inspection.*[19]

When I made my first request for information in 1997, the adoption agency cited Florida Statute 63.162 as the legal reason they couldn't release my records. The State didn't write this statute into law until October 1973 (seven months after my adoption). The legislation in 1971 addressed the confidentiality of records only. It did not guarantee the confidentiality of parties involved in the adoption proceedings, which appeared in part in the first writing of Florida Statute 63.162, *Hearings and Records in Adoption Proceedings*, as item four and only included the adoptive parents and the adopted child.[20]

> *Except as authorized in writing by the adoptive parent or the adopted child, if fourteen or more years of age, or upon order of the court for good cause shown in exceptional cases, no person is required to disclose the name or identity of either an adoptive parent or adopted child.*

Since its enactment, F.S. 63.162 has seen substantial change over time. The statute didn't explicitly protect the confidentiality of birth parents until 1978. The 1978 statute also included the stipulation to provide a birth family medical history to the adoptive parents before adoption.[21] The State later expanded the language to include all non-identifying information in 1982. The 1992 statute added a new section, *63.165 State Registry of Adoption Information; duty to inform and explain.* States created reunion registries as a passive means to allow birth family members the opportunity to connect by allowing anyone affected by adoption the ability to add their name to a database. Laurie did not make me aware of Florida's registry system (which did not exist in 1972) or my option to petition the court for good cause to let my birth parents know about the registry when I called in 1997. Surely my recent brush with breast surgery qualified as a "good cause." It was another six years before I joined the Florida Adoption Reunion Registry.

I realized years later that I was bound by the enacted law at the time of my request for information and not the statute under which Florida sealed my adoption. Full disclosure, I am not an attorney. The fact that adoption statutes appear to be applied retroactively doesn't make sense, and I couldn't find anything in the Florida Statutes that explicitly states adoption laws are retroactive. According to the United States Constitution, retroactive laws, referred to as ex post facto laws, are forbidden in criminal cases at the state and federal levels. Meaning that I couldn't be penalized for a legal action committed five years ago that has since been criminalized. Civil cases are fuzzier, but it's the punitive nature of ex post facto laws that make them unconstitutional. In the case of adoption, it is not a legal process that happens over time but an action that occurs at one point in time. By applying adoption law retroactively, a child adopted in March 1973, like me, received no benefits from changes in adoption statutes over time but was penalized by added restrictions.

When I made my first request for information in 1997, the added benefits in the current adoption statute not included at the time of my adoption were:

- Furnishing of all non-identifying information prior to the finalization of the adoption (1978 and 1982).
- Duty to inform birth parents prior to a relinquishment and adoptive parents prior to the adoption of the existence of the state reunion registry (1992).

And the added restrictions were:

- Inclusion of the original birth certificate as part of the adoption record (1977).
- Protection of natural parents' confidentiality (1978).

- Written authorization from birth parents prior to the release of their identity (1980).
- Payment by adoptees for release of their adoption information (1982).

I represent an adoptee who received the least number of benefits and the most amount of restrictions from the Florida Adoption Statute. The onus fell to me to understand adoptee rights and Florida law.

October 2013

For fifteen years, my search ebbed and flowed. I came back to my long list of Katherines from time to time and slowly crossed one name off and then another. I learned of 23andMe, a direct-to-consumer DNA test that provided me with ancestral and health information. My results revealed nothing earth-shattering except an Alzheimer's variant. I would likely lose my memory before figuring out who gave me the gene. My closest family match was a distant relative who may have shared a great-great-grandparent on either side.

March 2017

I whittled down my list of Katherines to one potential birth mother. My career path took me from being primarily a design engineer to a research engineer, and I honed my skills over the years. My research felt solid. I found Katherine based on several assumptions, and everything seemed to fit. You could now find many yearbooks online, and her high school pictures looked like me—nose, dimples, hair. I found a photo of her in a seated position and became fixated on her legs. She had a thin frame, like mine. But those thighs!

The size of my legs was a huge source of frustration for my mom. She referred to my legs as "soccer legs," claiming that finding clothes to fit me would be much easier if I didn't play the sport. It was true—I was hard to shop for. My thin waist usually didn't align with the cut of the pants that were supposed to fit around my big, muscular legs. I always had to size up where the pants' waistband settled around my hip bones. I'd obsessed over my traits. Until I saw that photo of my birth mother, it had never occurred to me that my thick legs were an inherited trait that soccer made more prominent.

Tracing this one Katherine to a Francis seemed to make many of the details, like birth parent ages, from my non-identifying information report line up. Katherine and Francis were from the same town and could have known each other. From an obituary found online, I confirmed that Katherine's father was a retired military man. But not all the information from my report lined up exactly. Some of the sibling names and ages were off. The report was described as hard to decipher, and I chalked it up to transcription errors.

One night over pink drinks adorned with red licorice swirls, I told my friends everything I knew about my birth parent discovery. *Yes*, they all agreed. *They must be THE Katherine and THE Francis.* I couldn't find the current contact information for Katherine. Still, Francis was easy enough to find—he worked as an engineer at a Boston university and had a public profile on the university's website. I was in the middle of asking for advice on whether I should reach out to Francis when the same friend who accompanied me on my Boston search a decade earlier insisted I let her reach out to him on my behalf. She had been with me throughout my journey and had recently discovered that she had an older brother. She had always assumed she was the oldest child of her parents because her mom never told her that she had a baby two years before marrying her dad. Her mom gave that baby up for adoption. She was shocked by the news but excited that her brother finally had the opportunity to meet their mom.

I wasn't sure what I wanted to do, but whatever it was, I felt comfortable having my best friend be my mouthpiece. She understood my journey, having been on the receiving end of the same news I was getting ready to deliver. Reaching out to a stranger may be the only definitive proof I may ever get to confirm my birth story—a mysterious child wanting to make connections. But I had always imagined that my first point of contact would be my birth mother. My non-identifying information painted my birth father as someone who didn't care enough to help his pregnant girlfriend. Would he feel differently more than forty years later? What if he denied the story, or worse, what if he never answered? Could I deal with that rejection all over again?

It took another fancy drink before I relented, and two weeks later, she sent an email. I don't know what my friend sent to Francis—I asked her not to share it with me. It didn't matter. We never heard back from him. Like all plans hatched in a bar, it seemed like a good idea at the time.

This experience with Francis made me think about accountability in adoption confidentiality. Maybe all parties agreed to have their identity sealed as part of my closed adoption. Perhaps it was a choice, maybe not. I tried to think of another aspect of life where we are not held accountable—where one could legally hide from actions that affect others. If I commit a crime, I am held accountable. If I accidentally damage someone's property, I am held accountable. If I make a mistake at work, I am held accountable. But if I have a baby, I can sign my rights away and pretend it never happened. I can deny my child the right to know where they came from, a right that is automatic for other children a birth parent chooses to raise. I know my story, my history, exists. Whose right does it become to control the information? Do I ever get the chance to grow up and claim my identity, the one that was rightfully mine when I was born?

The United States remains the only United Nations member country not to ratify the Convention on the Rights of the Child, an agreement made by countries promising to protect children. Ratification requires a two-thirds majority vote in the Senate but has failed to pass due to concerns over sovereignty and the ability of states to govern themselves. States control adoption laws, and legislation outlining access to closed records varies, typically falling into one of four categories: unrestricted access, access with restrictions, partial access, or sealed (as in the case of Florida).[22] Ratification of the Convention would require all states to amend their confidentiality laws and allow adoptees unrestricted access to their adoption records to comply with Article 8. Simply stated:

> *Children have the right to their own identity—an official record of who they are which includes their name, nationality and family relations. No one should take this away from them, but if this happens, governments must help children to quickly get their identity back.*[23]

What about my identity is so dangerous that Florida keeps it a state secret?

When I had the opportunity to meet a civil circuit judge from Mississippi, I was surprised to learn that closed adoptions still take place today. I asked her about closed adoptions, and she said that she still had several closed cases come through her courtroom. Her impression was that confidentiality was extremely important to the birth parents and that without it, there would be a rise in abortions. I can't say that I or the adoption research agrees with her. Domestic adoptions have declined since the 1960s. The standard practice for adoptions today in the United States is open arrangements, with only an estimated 5% of all adoptions being closed. Many people wrongly assume that if closed adoptions aren't an option, people who choose not to keep their children will turn to abortion. However, the choice to parent or not to parent influences abortions, not adoption secrecy. Women who do not want to parent typically choose abortion, not adoption. Of the women with unplanned pregnancies who choose to give birth, 99% opt to keep their babies.[24,25]

The challenges posed by closed adoption highlight the intent behind a system designed to protect the adopted child's best interests. Open domestic adoption is the gold standard because of healthier outcomes for adoptees and birth parents.[26] Each arrangement looks different, but at its core is an open exchange of information between all parties before and after adoption. The U.S. Department of Health and Human Services recognizes the benefits of open arrangements because the secrecy of closed adoption suggests something bad or shameful about the child's past.[27] But closed adoption files remain sealed in Florida and many other states. The legal system prevents the adoptee access to their past.

When do the adopted child's interests begin to outweigh those of the birth parent or adoptive parent or a system of retroactively applied statutes? When the adopted child expresses their desire to know more, will anyone hear them? When the adopted child wants to talk about their experience, will we listen?

EIGHT

Approximately 30,000 children are adopted across national borders each year, with the United States being the country with the largest number of internationally adopted children. Most of these adoptions are transracial, meaning the child becomes a visible minority in their own family, a unique and alienating experience. The age at which these children are brought to the United States varies between infants to teenagers, resulting in different levels of experience with their home and culture prior to adoption. Maintaining this connection with their culture is dependent on their parents' willingness to make that effort, especially in the early years of their adoption. As children adopted from China and brought to America, my brother and I are two of those 30,000 children. No matter how many people ask, neither of us have any memories of our lives in China as we were two years old when we were adopted. My parents did their best to provide us with cultural enrichment through traditions and food. However, it never filled that hole; I still felt like I was missing something that I can never get back. Children adopted from different cultures are disconnected from their identities due to the lack of opportunities to better understand and appreciate their biological roots…

My daughter called with the exciting news that she received 100% on her first college essay. The teacher pulled her aside after class to let her know that she rarely assigns a perfect score. She should be proud of herself.

The phone call caught me off guard. News about her successes usually comes by way of an email from a coach or teacher or by a mysterious text sent from an unknown number, presumably another parent who heard through their kid. Eva is an exceptional child, but she doesn't willingly volunteer information that makes her light shine any brighter. She prefers hanging out in the dark corner, going unnoticed. Extracting information from her is a painful experience easier had in the dentist's chair getting two root canals at once without Novocain. Communication is a dance that she has not yet perfected. She wants all her words to be precise, shaping each conversation to ensure no one's feelings are hurt. Not surprisingly, my request to read her paper was met with, "Um," long pause, "er," long pause, "uh," long pause, before she finally admitted, "it's about my adoption."

I had gone overboard with adoption information for my two kids. If I got nothing, they would get everything—not that there was much more to give. We didn't have any birth family information. My children were reportedly abandoned and found by strangers. Still, we received a treasure trove of material from the moment they were brought to their respective orphanages until they entered our lives. I handmade each a Lifebook, a children's storybook that illustrated their unique adoption journey, and a 400-page companion book that contained every shred of documentation about their adoption. Drawing on my experience as an adoptee and what I needed, I provided frequent parental check-ins to field any adoption questions. Neither seemed particularly interested in their adoption, or that is what I had always believed.

> *Due to the lack of an inherent connection with their culture, internationally adopted children must build that bridge themselves. Usually, people learn about their own culture just by living it; it is second nature to them. For many families, celebrating traditional holidays, eating traditional food, and wearing traditional clothes is expected. In high school, I noticed my friends' relationships with their cultures and how that differed from my experience, despite being a person of color just like them. They all had connections to their culture through their parents and grandparents, and I felt jealous of that because I was missing that connection in my own life…*

I had to remind myself that my daughter was writing about herself and not me. We were both adopted, and we were each experiencing an identity crisis of sorts, but hers was rooted more in culture. I vividly remember when a government official first placed Qiong Hua in my arms. Her bottom lip gave only a hint of a quiver, and I watched as her eyes darted around the room for a familiar face as if to ask, *What is happening to me?* In a room filled with crying babies, she was silent, stoic. I had been presented with a child who not only shared my dimples (as seen from photos showing a smiling baby in happier moments) but an attitude to match. At that moment, I could only see our similarities—what I was gaining and not what she was losing.

She was fifteen months old when we met, and ours would be her third known home, a home located on the other side of the world in a different country. Now at eighteen, she was opening up about the bridge she was building, a structure with missing blueprints, a structure I couldn't help her build because I am not Chinese.

> *To bridge that gap, my parents made it a tradition to celebrate Chinese New Year every year. My dad would stop by Chinatown after work to buy duck, sticky rice in banana leaves, and red bean pastries. However, as I began to learn more about Chinese culture, I discovered the inconsistencies between the significance of the traditions and the nonsensical decisions from my uneducated parents. Although I appreciated the effort my parents made to give my brother and me a "Chinese" experience, it highlighted the extra step that I had to take to receive the same cultural experience that my friends had since they were born. My junior year of high school, I fell in love with a fantasy Chinese drama about ancient martial arts. To enhance my understanding, I dove deep into the fandom to interact with fellow people who also enjoyed the show. Many of these people were Asian Americans with an abundance of knowledge of Chinese history and literature.*

> *They used this knowledge to further translate the show and all its details into something more than just the subtitles on the screen. I felt like a kid in a candy store, staring in awe at all the colorful information at my fingertips. I reached for the rich chocolate of history, and I carefully examined the complex swirls of pop culture…*

My heart sank as I read and realized that this was the part Eva probably felt most uncomfortable with her parents reading. She viewed our attempt at providing culture as nonsensical, and she didn't want to upset us. As an adoptee, I felt trained to help her navigate her experience, and I had failed her. What did I know about being Chinese? At the heart of any adoption is loss, and we both lost family and our identity. But her experience was exacerbated by the loss of an entire country.

> *Unfortunately, an adoptee's claim to culture is entirely dependent on their parents' attitudes toward bicultural socialization. Generally, parents fall into one of the three categories of attitudes towards their child's cultural belonging. Parents of the first group choose to completely deny any connection to a previous country, aiming to erase all history before their involvement. The second group is the opposite; parents are actively in contact with the birth family and live multiculturally. The third group's attitude is a mix of the two, based on the adoptee's comfort and curiosity. The parents adapt to their child's questions and acknowledge the complexity of their feelings about multiculturalism. I am lucky*

that this is the category that my parents fall into. I will admit, I shot myself in the foot with my childhood apathy. As young children, my parents enrolled both my brother and I into Chinese school. However, no one wants to sit at cramped desks memorizing numbers on a Saturday morning as a seven-year-old, so we quit after a few years. Since my mom's own adoption was a glaring unknown in her life, she was especially conscientious about multiculturalism. She strived to be completely transparent about our adoptions, consistently initiating conversations checking in on my feelings about my experience. I, allergic to discussing feelings, especially when I was younger, only truly started appreciating these opportunities when I was in high school, and it was too late to take advantage of any of them. No matter the parents' views on biculturalism, all international adoptees must form their own connections with their own cultures…

Eva eloquently captured what is so challenging to articulate as an adoptee—how parent attitudes can drive the adoption experience. And Eva being Eva, not wanting to step directly on anybody's toes, did it without being overly critical of any one path. The categories she outlined could be applied to my own experience and the United States' history with closed, open, and semi-open adoption arrangements. For me, society, and by default, my parents, chose to deny me any connection to my previous life by opting for a closed adoption. While I was happy to read that Eva felt lucky for her perceived semi-open adoption experience, I wish I could have given her more.

Transracial adoptees typically feel out of place in both the country they were born in and the country in which they reside. Granted, this is not a feeling that is unique to transracial adoptees; it is shared with mixed-race people who also have feet in multiple cultures. However, it differs by virtue of mixed people having that inherent connection with their cultures through their parents that adoptees lack. I feel strange calling myself Asian American because my experiences are not Asian American. One of the most common mircoaggressions against Asian Americans is being mocked at school for the food that their parents cooked for lunch. Since my parents do not cook these traditional foods, I did not have this issue. Being unable to participate in these types of conversations makes me feel as though my experience, and therefore identity, as a Chinese American is inauthentic. In fact, I remember being so excited when I slept over at my second-generation Chinese friend's house and joined her during family meals because it was a glimpse into what an Asian American household is like. We were given small bowls of rice and took portions of cooked vegetables and fish from the middle to put into our bowls. The most novel part of the whole meal for me was that it was for breakfast! Eating traditional food is an essential pillar when developing a strong cultural identity. Other pillars include learning the language, participating in holidays, and becoming aware of one's physical similarities with those of the same country. For adoptees, it is difficult to build these pillars, resulting in an unsteady sense of cultural identity. This unsteadiness can spread to other aspects of a person's life, often manifesting in depression or anxiety. Even though my Chinese identity is teetering at best, I am still not white, as my physical appearance constantly reminds me…

I recently finished reading *All You Can Ever Know* by Nicole Chung. The memoir was beautifully written and spoke directly to my heart as a domestic adoptee and as someone who adopted children transracially from another country. The book was a national bestseller and received critical acclaim. The negative reviews it received were few but almost as noteworthy because I am curious about what others (seemingly not adopted) feel about a personal adoption narrative written by an adoptee. Common threads of distorted perspectives prevail—that families can be built on unconditional love alone, that the adoptee experience is inauthentic unless adoptive parents or the sacrifices of others are acknowledged, and that adoptees are unhappy if they don't openly recognize all that they were given. Adoptees MUST be grateful and bury their loss deep inside, or they are subject to a one-star review and labeled "self-centered" or "whiney."

Being adopted comes with many realizations that shift an individual's entire worldview. Many adoptees do not have any connection with their birth parents. As a result, the first few years of their lives, one of the most formative times for young children, is a period characterized by unknowns. These unknowns leave people vulnerable to world-changing moments of understanding when introduced to new knowledge. I finally registered the fact that I was adopted when I was in third grade. For a few months, it was all I would talk about. I even made a small presentation for my class. The novelty eventually wore off, and my adoption became something I only talked about with my closest friends. A few years ago, I witnessed my brother go through the same realization that I had. He became obsessed with China and being Chinese, just like I did. The curiosity is only understandable; finding out I am from a different place than the one I have been a part of as far as I remember is both jarring and fascinating. I vividly remember the moment I found out that I do not know my actual birthdate. I was talking with my mom about what she knew about her adoption, and she mentioned being issued an amended birth certificate that had her date and time of birth noted. My brother had been left with a note that disclosed his date and time of birth. I was left with nothing. Something did not click. If I didn't have a birth certificate or a note from my birth parents, then how did I know my birthday? My mom told me that doctors probably estimated it based on the condition of my umbilical cord and therefore, I could have been born on a different day than I thought I was my entire life. In the moment, I remember dismissing it as no big deal, but it has stuck with me like an ominous cloud. A seemingly insignificant effect is through my interest in astrology. I am not on the cusp but being born a week earlier would make the difference between being a Sagittarius or a Scorpio. For a few months after the realization, I felt as if I did not have a claim to being a Sagittarius.

Some of my friends know much more about astrology than I do, and through them, I have become aware of so much more than just my sun sign. However, knowing my birth time is required for many of these aspects, including the rising sign, one of the big three. Reading my horoscope, there is always a little voice in my head whispering that there is no way it is accurate because I have the wrong information. It is unsettling and destabilizing to have these reminders constantly in the back of my mind…

It bothers me that Eva doesn't know her exact birthdate. My in-laws insisted that she must be older than what was reported because she was advanced compared to her cousins, their biological grandkids. If she was older, it couldn't be by more than a month based on her size and growth. Some kids walk at eight months and some at twelve months. What does a month matter? And why was it so crucial for my in-laws to acknowledge it?

A birthdate is an inherent birthright—something that a birth parent passes to their child and something my husband and I couldn't give our daughter. Although amended, I had a birth certificate, and no one ever questioned my birthdate. It was a date I took for granted until I later learned that some adoptees found discrepancies in their birth information—sometimes the result of a simple transcription error from one document to the next and sometimes the result of something more sinister. What if one of the few things I had always believed to be true was not? My reported birthdate lands on an astrology cusp. Am I still me if I fell under a different sign?

I wish I could give my daughter what my son was given, a tiny breadcrumb to her past—a handwritten note from her birth parents, a note expressing both their sorrow for being too poor to raise her and their love by acknowledging her birth.

Transracially adopted children have the complicated experience of being separated from the very culture they were born in, resulting in an unsteady sense of identity. An individual's cultural identity is a significant part of how they perceive themselves and having to construct it for oneself can have significant effects. While I am lucky to have such understanding parents, that does not mean those effects do not influence who I am today. The empty hole that was created when I left China will most likely never be filled, but I can strive to complete it the best I can. Even if I ever did find my birth parents and was able to get answers to many of my questions, I know it would be different in ways I could never predict. That is just another unknown that is a side effect of being adopted.

-*Eva Qiong Hua,* "Building Better Bridges"

NINE

"There are significant questions surrounding the reliability of Changsha's finding information."[28]

My daughter and I were adopted at the end of two adoption booms—me, the Baby Scoop Era, and her, China's international adoption program. The possibility that both of our stories originated in systems rife with secrecy and coercive tactics seemed implausible. The fact that I unknowingly perpetuated a system that I admonished was a hard pill to swallow.

To combat crippling population growth, China initiated its One Child Policy in 1979, allowing each family to have only one child. This policy was formally written into China's Constitution in 1982 and strictly enforced until 2015, when the policy ended, allowing each family to have two children per household. When census data showed a decline in birth rates in 2021, China raised the quota to three children. It was an oversimplified solution to help control the population and a policy that came with unintended consequences.

My husband and I bought into the widespread belief that international adoption programs were established to help reduce a burgeoning population of children in China's welfare institutions and the theory behind why so many baby girls were being abandoned—a country's cultural preference for boys. China scholar Kay Ann Johnson's research exposes a more complex problem—that the out-of-plan child is "born with an exorbitant price on its head."[29] Being born to Chinese citizens in China doesn't guarantee a child household registration, citizenship, or the entitlements that both bring and being born in violation of China's birth policy obligated families to pay hefty fines for non-compliance or face other stiff penalties, such as a forced abortion or sterilization, property destruction, and even seizure of their child by local birth planning officials. Children ended up in welfare institutions even when their families wanted to keep them or extended family or friends agreed to adopt them domestically. At our adoption in February 2005, China's international program generated more revenue than domestic adoption. The decreasing number of children available for adoption and the fees international families were willing to pay was the perfect storm for corruption to breed.

In November 2005, news broke in Hunan, China, about suspected child trafficking to feed its lucrative international adoption program. The initial story included my daughter's orphanage in Changsha, an institution with a sizeable international adoption program and one that China's government later cleared of any wrongdoing. Eva had been adopted through China's healthy child program, a popular international program in the early 2000s. We felt we had done our research, and adoption agencies billed China as one of the most stable and transparent international adoption programs. We selected an agency with a long, rich history in adoption and cultural and humanitarian programs. When we were required to bring an orphanage donation of $3,000 in crisp U.S. twenty-dollar bills, we didn't question its validity. Our daughter's care wasn't free—the money was reportedly used to help fund the welfare institution. The U.S. government regulated China's international adoption program, and we went through a lengthy process of required procedures before being approved.

There was no easy way to make an adoption plan in China, and many of the babies that ended up in orphanages were reportedly abandoned. Prior to the adoption of any Chinese child, the orphanage is required to publish a finding ad in a local newspaper to allow birth parents to reclaim their child. Finding ads typically list the child's finding location, approximate age, and physical description and unintentionally became a tool to compile abandonment data. Changsha's finding data revealed that our daughter's orphanage likely used financial incentives to lure children into the institution.[30] Orphanages participating in these practices utilized an organized network of "traffickers" who were paid a finder's fee for each child. After the 2005 media exposure, the number of abandoned children being found on the streets of Changsha dropped significantly, an indication that not all children's abandonments were legitimate. Given the size of the city, Eva's finding location was not unique. She was one of five children found at the same spot in the same year, and there were variations in her abandonment reporting—most notably which police station brought her to the orphanage. Eva may have arrived at the Changsha Social Welfare Institute by way of a trafficker for financial gain, her paperwork fabricated to qualify her for international adoption. Eva may have been a wanted child who fell victim to government policies and coercive tactics that landed her in America to be raised by a white couple.

The United States was not immune to its own adoption scandals. There was the Magdalene Laundries of Ireland, which supplied wealthy Americans with an estimated 2,000 babies forcibly taken from their unwed birth mothers. There was Dr. Thomas Hicks, a physician who ran a medical clinic in McCaysville, Georgia, who illegally sold more than 200 babies for adoption out of his clinic's back door. But one of the most notable cases is that of Georgia Tann, a social worker who ran the Tennessee Children's Home Society in Memphis.[31] She kidnapped an estimated 5,000 children and sold them for adoption. Georgia Tann successfully commercialized adoption in the 1930s and 1940s by advertising available children nationally and selling them to famous people, such as actor Joan Crawford. Tann was also successful at influencing adoption law. She falsified birth records with the intent to cover her crimes. She then sold her practice of the "amended" birth certificate to state legislators, billing it as a way to protect the child from the stigma of illegitimacy. All fifty states ultimately passed laws to seal original birth certificates, including then-New York Governor Herbert Lehman, who bought two babies from Tann.[32]

My husband and I were a few months into the application process for our second healthy child adoption when the 2005 trafficking concerns prompted us to switch to China's special needs program. The reasons behind a child's abandonment for a special need were more apparent than for an "out-of-plan" child that broke the country's One Child Policy. A child through this program would likely have been abandoned by their parents because of a medical need. But we learned that their stories are no less tragic.

We adopted a boy born with a significant cleft lip and palate. Western countries don't consider this need a big deal because surgeries can correct the malformation, and insurance is available to pay the expense. But low-income families in China don't have the same access to medical care, and they are left with the overwhelming burden of adequately caring for a child with little resources.

Our son was found the same day he was born and transferred to a local orphanage, where he lived until his adoption at age two. I imagine that had he been born in the United States, he would have developed into a healthy adult. But an institution is a harsh environment for someone who needs extra care to survive, and the damage his circumstance caused will have life-long effects. The flat spot on his head indicated neglect, not because nobody cared but because the baby-tocaregiver ratio was too high for proper care. His wide cleft exacerbated his ability to feed adequately—he needed extra time and nourishment, neither of which were available. The orphanage provided the initial surgeries to close the cleft, but the emotional cost was high. Our son was left at the hospital by orphanage staff and endured the post-operative pain without the benefit of medication or someone to hold his hand.

When my husband and I first met our son in China, there were indications that the road forward would be challenging. We had no idea what our future held because the orphanage didn't disclose any need outside of his cleft before our arrival. We had the option of declining his adoption and leaving him behind in China. *Leave my child behind?* Would this same option be presented if I had given birth to him? We were committed to our child and his care, and we brought him home. At age three, doctors diagnosed him on the Autism Spectrum. At seven, epilepsy developed. But the most profound effect of his early life presents as Post Traumatic Stress Disorder. The brain can't always recover from trauma.

The unknowns surrounding adoption raises many ethical questions. Was I better off in my adoptive family? Were my children better off in America? How do you measure opportunity? As a child with an illegitimate stigma or as a child with amended documents that make them legitimate? As an unregistered second or third child in China without rights or as an Asian child growing up in a western country fraught with racism? As a child growing up in the culture and family they were born into or as a child with access to quality health care and education? If my husband and I found out that Eva was forcibly taken from her birth parents, would we be willing to give her back to an unfamiliar family and country? If we knew the extent of our son's needs and the emotional toll it would take on our lives, would we have agreed to the adoption before we arrived in China? I want to say, "Yes." It feels like the correct answer.

What I know to be true is that my birth story is being held hostage by a legal system. If adoption laws change, there may be a point in time where I can learn about my beginnings. However, my children's birth story does not exist in any document or court. Their story exists only in their bones.

TEN

I learned about my mom through an Instagram photo with the caption, "the rain & the sun on a bright dark day." I knew what it meant. My brother posted an image he snapped on his way back home after responding to my dad's frantic, late-night call. He arrived at our childhood home to find police on the scene and my dad waiting outside in the driveway. It was not uncommon for my mom to sleep in twelve-hour blocks thanks to a cocktail of Vicodin and Ambien, but when time stretched into the fifteenth hour, my dad went to check on his wife. He found her cold. She was dead. It had taken her three tries.

My mom left behind three suicide notes. I read them after the police released them from their small evidence pile. She was unhappy. Her life was not perfect. Her kids were not perfect. Her grandkids were not perfect. Each rambling page left me wondering if she was talking about the same life I'd witnessed her living. The one where her daughter earned a Ph.D. and her two sons were successful businessmen at major corporations? The one where her doting husband diligently saved more than enough retirement funds to travel around the world with her multiple times over? The one where she ran a successful interior decorating business for decades? The one where she had seven amazing and talented grandchildren?

My mom wrestled with untreated mental illness for many years. Retirement left her brain with too much unoccupied space. She filled it with negative thoughts and medicated them with a rainbow of pills. She blamed us for her demise. We were not perfect.

I am not perfect.

I am not good enough.

I killed my mom.

I killed her desire to live.

Who am I?

I entered the world with my very own genetic marker, information passed on to me by my birth parents. Deoxyribonucleic acid, or DNA—it's what makes me, scientifically me.

The ability to sequence DNA of the entire human genome was a breakthrough in genetic science that advanced through the 1990s with the Human Genome Project. In 2008, *TIME* magazine named 23andMe's Personal Genome Service as its "Invention of the Year." The world of affordable direct-to-consumer (DTC) DNA testing was becoming accessible to the average person. By 2017, AncestryDNA emerged as the leader in personal genetic testing accounting for the majority of collected samples from any one company.[33,34] The saliva sample I sent to 23andMe almost four years earlier still had no viable genetic relative to trace to a possible birth parent. After my failed attempt at a Francis connection, I decided to send more of "me" to the company with the most extensive database. In June 2017, I received my results from AncestryDNA—two close family matches.

Affordable genetic testing is the unforeseen confidentiality loophole in the closed adoption system, and technological advances in genome sequencing bring into question the perpetuation of sealed adoption records. While states have the power to regulate adoption laws and records, the world of DTC DNA testing remains largely unregulated. With the use of Ancestry's Matches and 23andMe's Relatives tools, DNA is connecting adoptees and birth families—sometimes surreptitiously and sometimes knowingly, such as through the pro bono project of DNA Quest (now facilitated by MyHeritage) that allows adoptees and birth family members to upload their DNA for purposes of making connections.[35] The new field of genetic genealogy has expanded genealogical research beyond historical documents to include science and the genetic material that connects families.

Not surprisingly, people have raised privacy questions about DTC DNA testing. When an individual consents and uploads genetic information about themselves, for genealogy research, for medical insights, or for other reasons, they indirectly consent for others who share their DNA, others who may want to stay hidden.[36, 37] The recent capture of the Golden State Killer is an example used when talking about privacy concerns. In this case, investigators covertly uploaded crime scene DNA to both public and private databases to eventually find a match. The Golden State Killer's family was ultimately responsible for his capture without their knowledge.

Genetic testing introduces ethical concerns, particularly where the line gets drawn—who can access DNA and why? The Pew Research Center estimates that roughly half of Americans are okay with their genetic information being shared with law enforcement.[38] I would allow the use of my DNA if I knew it would be used for the greater good. But I thought long and hard before giving up my DNA profile to a database that many people can access. I heard stories of private insurance companies using people's genetic information against them to deny medical treatment and coverage. I didn't want to expose myself to any future risk. But I had reached only dead ends in my search, and DTC DNA was my last resort. My intense desire to find my birth family won out. What other choice did I have?

The two companies that have my profile have strict privacy policies, but at no time have I understood my information to be protected. Thanks to the digital age, my medical information, biometrics data, and likely many other personal records exist on computer servers that are all vulnerable. Before that, my information existed in paper files that agencies and institutions could easily mishandle. My social security number was my college ID, with the number printed boldly on my card under my photo. Was any of my personal information ever secure? Did I ever really have any control?

Regulatory oversight of DTC DNA data may be needed to help address privacy concerns. But if privacy is the perceived right to control one's own information, what happens when that same information impacts others? A criminal or their family may feel violated by third-party use of DNA for identification, but do they have a right to stay hidden when others have suffered? A birth parent may want to remain anonymous, but do they have the right to deny all relationships others might desire? The information that someone can gain from DNA can play a pivotal role in their understanding of circumstance and self. Genetic genealogy can mean the difference between life and death.

For law enforcement, consumer DNA databases have been able to crack cases long gone cold. The Golden State Killer was caught four decades after committing his first known crime. A Long Island woman's persistent effort to persuade detectives to consider searching consumer DNA to help identify the person who murdered her sister in 1980 finally paid off in 2022. Consumer DNA databases expand the FBI's Combined DNA Index System (CODIS) beyond genetic material collected at crime scenes. When used responsibly, as an investigative tool under established guidelines, DTC DNA can help catch killers and identify missing and unidentified crime victims.

For adoptees, DTC DNA testing opens new doors of discovery. Medical professionals often interpret our unknown family medical history as having no family history of any diseases. After reading the story of a twenty-five-year-old adoptee diagnosed with breast cancer, I could almost place myself in her shoes.[39] No one could have suspected that a woman so young had breast cancer. Her symptoms went undiagnosed until a doctor finally ordered genetic testing that revealed she carried the BRCA1 gene. The gene mutated into cancer, and she later died. Still, the information prompted testing of her young daughter, who was also a carrier of the gene. Armed with information, the daughter will start breast cancer screening at age sixteen. DTC DNA testing provides adoptees with valuable health information that was previously unknown. For me, it also provided a new lead.

My first connection to my birth family was through a first cousin on my birth mother's side. She knew about me, and my initial contact with her was met with an overload of information. "Hello! Yes, I know EXACTLY who you are!!" was followed by three lengthy chats fired one after the other through AncestryDNA's message service. She included all the information she thought I should know and even more. I instantly fell in love with her.

The information I received was overwhelming. I had gone from knowing nothing about my past to being handed the names, ages, and locations of most of my birth mother's family in a matter of minutes. I would see many of them for the first time after cyber-stalking their social media feeds for photos. My new cousin emailed me a picture of my birth mother and her siblings standing side-by-side at a recent family function. I studied that photo, trying to find my face among the five strangers looking back at me. I couldn't. They all looked different from each other, and they all looked different from me. If I found a photo of my birth mother in a high school yearbook years earlier, would I have dismissed it? Staring at the face that bears no resemblance to mine and at the last name that I would have mistaken to be Jewish made me think that I might have done just that.

The focus of my search had been finding my birth mother's last name. The name I was now staring at was unmistakably German (the first of two ethnicities reported by the adoption agency) and none of the Katherines I had been researching for the past twenty years. Before I had time to think about how this name missed every search parameter, I thought back to the email sent a few months earlier to Francis. A Francis that I connected to a different Katherine. A Katherine that was not my birth mother according to DNA. I now wondered what he thought about receiving an email in his work's inbox reporting that he could be the father of a baby produced in his youth. "Oopsie, my bad," may have been the appropriate subject line of a follow-up email to Francis that included a heartfelt apology explaining that I had identified the wrong guy as my birth father. But I only shrugged and thought that maybe every guy should receive this type of letter. I couldn't feel sorry that the message had been sent. Maybe Francis would be sympathetic to the lengths I had gone through to find him. Maybe he would be thankful for DTC DNA technology.

Nine months after my mom's death, I would see my birth mother again for the first time since she kissed my forehead and handed me over to the hospital nurse. Our meeting seemed timed as if my two mothers knew they could never occupy the same space.

ELEVEN

Dear Katherine,

I have wanted to meet you most of my life. I can't imagine how hard it must have been to make that painful decision of giving me up for adoption. I am not sure how to adequately summarize the last 44 years of my life except to say that I have had a great life. It is my hope that this letter is only the beginning of us getting to know one another.

I have always been very curious about where I came from. In my mid-20s, I was able to obtain non-identifying birth family information from the adoption agency. That helped paint a picture but in very broad strokes. It was then that I started the serious search to find you. And so here we are…

It seemed strange to type out a letter to the woman who gave me life as if I were conducting a simple business transaction. I must have written my birth mother a thousand times already in my mind. But committing to words in a letter that may never be read seemed convoluted, a torturous exercise.

Through my cousin, who'd quickly become an intermediary, I found out that my birth mother was excited I'd made contact. The thought of my birth mother not wanting to talk to me was a possibility—one I'd heard about in other adoption reunions. But I was part her, and her part me. I couldn't fathom giving up a child and not wanting to know if they were okay in this world. It felt good to know that my birth mother felt the same.

My family was excited to hear about my birth mother connection. I didn't even read through all the details my cousin sent through Ancestry's message service before I picked up the phone to tell my husband the news. I exchanged a flurry of texts with my dad and brothers in a group chat so that everyone heard the announcement at the same time (because if you ever prioritized one person over another, you heard about it for the next year and a half).

Kacie: After 20 years of searching, I now know who my birth mother is through DNA!

Jeff: Wow!!!!! Who is she?

Dad: Is she the same one that you were starting to suspect up in New England?

Kacie: I was all wrong! Connected with a first cousin who knew about me, and she gave me a name. She seems excited to help make connections.

Danny: Just talked to Kacie. AMAZING story… and it is just the first chapter! (I got that off the Hallmark website :-)

Later in the day, I forwarded all the messages and the family photo sent by my cousin to my family.

Danny: Great stuff. Your birth mother and her siblings all look different from one another. I see you in the group of sisters. Some of the upper body parts seem similar... Jeff probably has a tactful way of elaborating.

Jeff: I'd recognize that nose anywhere (Dan, is that what you were referring to? :-)

Danny: Using the word voluptuous didn't seem appropriate in a text about my sister :-)

Dad: I was touched by the comment about this connection being one of the happiest days for their family.

As great as my dad is at ignoring his kid's inappropriate humor, he is the one of us who couldn't be bothered with rules or proper etiquette. He lives by the adage, "It's better to ask forgiveness than permission." The forwarded messages came with my cousin's cell phone number and the statement, "Call or text anytime." I can see my dad latching on to that one statement as if my cousin were speaking directly to him and not me.

> **Richard:** I have resisted the temptation to contact you earlier because I felt it was important for the communication to be done by Kacie, but I wanted to pass on my heartfelt thanks and appreciation to you and to everyone in your family who is helping Kacie connect with her birth mother. Kacie has been such a wonderful blessing. I will never forget your first words to her, words she has wanted to hear for so long, "I know exactly who you are." God bless you and your family.

He admitted to reaching out only after receiving a return text. He knew I couldn't be mad at him for possibly overstepping his role in my reunion after I read my cousin's response.

> **Cousin:** It's so great to meet you, Richard! I can't thank you enough for reaching out to me and for the beautiful message you wrote me. I almost cried reading. I should be thanking YOU for the amazing life you and your late wife gave Kacie (and her brothers). She's expressed to me that you've surrounded her with love and supported her journey to finding her birth mother/relatives, and I couldn't be more grateful. She is such a positive, understanding person, and that's because of the wonderful upbringing you've provided. I hope to meet you in person to thank you for giving my cousin such a wonderful life! Thank you for making my day!!

He was right. I wasn't mad.

Two days after I'd emailed my letter (via intermediary), I received a reply from my birth mother in my inbox.

Hi Kacie,

I always hoped that you would try to find me, and here we are! I am so happy to hear that you had a great life. That is all I have ever wanted for you, and now that we are all adults, I can come to know you too. I'm looking forward with anticipation to meeting you (again) and getting to know you and your family.

Isn't it surreal that we are both Katherine?

One month later, we met (again).

TWELVE

Hi Katherine,

It was so great to talk to you tonight. I thought I was going to be overwhelmed and overly emotional, but it was like talking to an old friend. Is that strange? Please don't discount the fact that you created the amazing me. I can never thank you enough for that.

It seemed safe to communicate with my birth mother through email. I could write out my feelings and then edit to perceived perfection. When she asked if she could call me, I wasn't sure what to say. We would be meeting in person soon enough, and I wanted the entire picture of her all at once, not the piecemeal approach we were currently taking. We'd already started attaching photos to our email correspondence. Now she was asking to hear my voice and have a conversation. I wanted to touch her first. I needed validation that she was real, not just words, or a series of photos, or a voice. She was still a stranger to me, but I relented. I wanted to make her happy. I owed her that.

Adoption reunions reportedly go through stages. I knew this—twenty years of searching with too much waiting in-between gave me time to consume every possible adoption memoir and adoption reunion experience. In the book *Birthright*, Jean A.S. Strauss describes the stages as 1. Fantasy; 2. First Encounters; 3. The Morning After; 4. Limbo; and, 5. Reconciliation. [40] Reunions are an emotional roller coaster explained as excitement and obsession followed by confusion, disruption, and acceptance. It felt good coming armed with information. I will step around all the common pitfalls. My reunion experience will be different.

Fantasy

I lied a little when I said I didn't grow up fantasizing about my birth parents. True—my birth father was a blank slate. False—my birth mother was a blank slate. I'd hoped that my birth mother was Dolly Parton. She was talented and funny, and she made me smile. She made big boobs and country music cool (and I liked neither). Maybe she didn't have any kids because all she could do was mourn for the one she gave away. Whenever I saw *9 to 5* or heard *Islands in the Stream*, I found myself thinking, *Dolly, are you my birth mother?* If I just ignored the fact that she wasn't eighteen in 1972, this could be true.

My birth mother's fantasy was that someday she would open her door to find her firstborn, a curly redhead, on the other side. She'd remembered me being born with red hair, and when I sent her one of my toddler photos and a high school graduation photo that sepia touch up had tinted red, she couldn't be convinced otherwise.

First Encounters

I was surprised to find myself on a large Boeing 777 for my short 500-mile flight to North Carolina. Maybe the airlines got wind of my reunion and rolled out the biggest jet just for me. I was obsessed with airplanes—how they stayed up in the air, but mostly how sometimes they failed to stay up in the air. *What if I die in a plane crash before I meet her?*

I settled into my middle aisle seat, pulling out a book from my backpack, knowing I would only open it and stare at the bookmarked page. I was meeting my birth mother in approximately one hour, and my mind was racing. Up in the air, the woman next to me leaned over and asked if smoke was coming out of the air vents. I assured her that this sometimes happens on hot, humid days and that what looked like smoke was just water vapor. Engineers like to think they know everything about anything mechanical (because we do).

I imagined the woman sitting next to me traveling to see her daughter and grandchildren—it felt important to reassure her that she would get there safely. I imagined the woman placing a reassuring hand over mine. *Don't worry. You'll arrive safely too. You won't leave this world without finding out everything you desire.*

The remainder of my flight, touchdown, and the walk through the airport was a complete blur. I was on autopilot, following the lead of other passengers to the baggage terminal. My entire twenty-year search was leading to this one moment—being held by my birth mother for the first (second) time.

As I stepped outside and to curbside pickup, I saw her standing off at a distance, waiting for me. A big smile emerged on my face, and I waved to acknowledge her. She turned and looked in my direction, but she seemed puzzled, as if I had just waved to the wrong person by mistake. I was glad we exchanged so many photos in advance now because I was sure I was walking toward the right person. When I got closer, her smile grew, and relief settled over me. When I finally reached her, before any words were spoken, she enveloped me in a hug only a mother could give.

Her husband, who'd driven her to the airport, ushered us into the backseat of the car so we didn't have to separate. Two minutes in, and I already couldn't get enough of her. She was intoxicating, and I did my best to absorb everything about her before I had to let go.

When I made my initial plans to visit my birth mother, I reserved a hotel and a rental car. It seemed healthier to create some boundaries at the start. We could meet, and then I could retreat and process. This is normal Kacie behavior. But somewhere in the month between our first connection and our first meeting, the reservations were canceled. It was probably a mutual decision. I can't remember now. I was staying at their house with no means of escape. It seemed reckless to stay with strangers. Was Katherine a stranger? Admittedly, I Google Earthed their house in advance to make sure there was, in fact, a house at the address my birth mother gave me. It seemed like a perfectly normal neighborhood and not one where a serial killer would be hiding out. And when I met Katherine and her husband at the airport, they seemed like pleasant, normal people.

I spent the drive to their house curled up next to my birth mother in the back seat. I can't remember what we talked about, but I remember staring at her hands and feet. I already knew that our faces didn't match, and now I knew that our hands and feet didn't either. I had long, thin fingers and size nine shoes. She had petit hands and feet, and her sandals revealed toes that looked nothing like mine. Can DNA ever be wrong?

We pulled up to a little green house tucked against mature trees and shrubs. It was well kept with a classy assortment of lawn ornaments. Walking through the front door, I was hit with the smell of potpourri. It wasn't overpowering like a candle store, but it took me a second to adjust before moving further into the house. It was eclectically decorated, packed with many years of furnishings and knick-knacks that they couldn't bring themselves to let go of. They mentioned moving to North Carolina from the northeast a few years before to be closer to their kids and grandkids. This was their attempt at downsizing—a smaller house that had to accommodate the same amount of stuff. It was not my taste, but squashing my critical inner Joyce, I simply said, "You have a really nice house."

After a quick tour and a chance to freshen up, Katherine brought me to her study so we would be alone to talk. I sat down in a wingback chair next to her and across from an extensive collection of aging Raggedy Ann dolls. I settled in, prepared to have all the questions I have ever wanted answered, answered. But before I could ask the big one, "Who is my birth father?" a question I had reserved for our first face-to-face, Katherine saw me look over at the manila folder on the table between us and said, "Oh, I put that together for you. Take a look." I opened the folder expecting to find a stack of family photos that I could take home with me. What I found instead was a stack of typewritten papers. The top page was a list of names and dates going back to 1733. Katherine mentioned in a prior email that my seventh great-grandfather emigrated from Germany and later fought in the Revolutionary War. I quickly realized that this was that direct family line. She seemed excited about this genealogical revelation and thought to include it as the first thing I would see. "This is what you'll need if you are interested in becoming a member of the Daughters of the American Revolution." I didn't have the heart to tell her that it would be challenging for me to prove any legal identity to her family line (or that I had any interest in genealogy at this moment). With a smile on my face, I listened as she described each name on her paternal grandfather's branch of the family tree.

I continued to thumb through the file, which seemingly held only historical facts for the German side of the family. I stopped when Katherine said, "That's a tragic story." It was hard to miss the bold, all-cap headline of the *Allentown Democrat Newspaper* article from 1909, "Woman dies in arms of frantic husband, horribly burned." The story went on to describe the events of how Katherine's great-grandmother, Mary, was burned alive. Initially ruled an accident, a second article published a few days later alluded to something else. I thought it was a curious tidbit of family history to give your new-found daughter, but I went on to skim the article giving in to my morbid fascination of anything horrifying.

After a thorough investigation, the coroner concluded suicide by incineration. The facts of the case included Mary's repeated threats of suicide and the testimony of Mary's six-year-old daughter—how she witnessed her mother saturate her clothes with gasoline, light a match, and set herself on fire. Mary's son (Katherine's grandfather, who'd turn seven the following day) saw his mother run down the stairs from the second floor, completely engulfed in flames. Mary's husband grabbed his overcoat and wrapped it around his wife to try and extinguish the flames, becoming badly burned in the process.

Assuming no other typed piece of history that followed in the file would be as tragic (or fascinating), I closed the folder and put it back on the table. Not knowing what to do or say next, I sat back in the chair and stared at my audience of dolls on the other side of the room. Katherine broke the silence by asking, "What questions do you have for me?"

I wasn't sure how to approach the subject of my birth father. Up until now, she hadn't willingly offered any information, and she acted as if she had created me with no help. I brought with me an icebreaker of sorts that I hoped would help ease us into the delicate conversation. I leaned over and grabbed the bag I carried with me into the study and placed it on my lap. The first thing I pulled out was a baby outfit—the one my parents bought me for my journey home from the adoption agency. It was one of the few items of my youth that my mom kept, and I knew, even though she didn't support my decision to search, she would want me to pass it on to Katherine as a token of her thanks. I imagined her saying, "She's all yours now. Please take good care of our daughter." But before I handed over the outfit and explained its significance, I gave Katherine a handwritten letter from my dad.

July 15, 2017

Dear Katherine,

As you read this, you and Kacie will be together after almost 45 years! I am amazed at what Kacie has accomplished in her life, but I'm sure she counts finding you as one of her greatest blessings.

Placing Kacie for adoption back in 1972 was likely the most difficult decision of your life. I want you to know that your decision was the beginning of an amazing gift—for my wife, myself, and our family. It is my hope that as Kacie now shares her life with you, you will be blessed and that some of your pain will be erased.

Many years ago, Kacie added a special Bible verse to my birthday card. I extend this Bible verse to you so that you may be filled with joy during this special reunion.

"Now unto him that is able to keep you from falling, and to present you faultless before the presence of his glory with exceeding joy." (Jude 1:24)

Everyone in our family has been filled with immeasurable joy since June 9, when your niece replied to Kacie, "I know exactly who you are!" It is truly a connection guided by God.

God bless you!

Love,
Richard

Katherine was touched by the letter, and tears started to well up in her eyes before she reached the end. Her tears began to fall when I gave her my baby outfit. By the time I pulled the next gift out of my bag, a professional photo album of me spanning all the years she had missed, she was sobbing. I handed her the book and narrated it as she carefully flipped through so that her tears didn't spill onto its pages.

Thirty minutes later, I pulled out the last item from my bag, a copy of my non-identifying information report. Handing it to her, I said, "The adoption agency gave me this twenty years ago, and I would love for you to read it."

By the time she reached the end, her tears had dried up. "Yes, this is all true," she said curtly as she shifted her focus from the last page and back onto my face. This was my opportunity. "Can you tell me more about my birth father, Francis?"

THIRTEEN

Some of the first pieces of information relayed to me by my new cousin was that I had three half-siblings, a sister and two brothers. During my first phone conversation with Katherine, I asked her about her kids and if they knew about me. She told me that she never told her kids about me but that her husband always knew. She went on to say that her relationship with her kids was a complicated one and that she preferred to wait until we met in person to tell me more about them. She opened up more in a later phone call only to say that she and her daughter were currently estranged—that they had a misunderstanding and hadn't talked in a while. I didn't press her for more details. The thought of estrangement with one of her own children was hard to process, and a day later, I sent a follow-up email.

Hi Katherine,

I know that you prefer to talk by phone, but right now, it is easier for me to write the deeper stuff down. This will get easier for me as we get to know each other better.

I wanted to thank you for telling me about your daughter even though you wanted to wait until I was in North Carolina.

This issue was really weighing on me, and I appreciate your willingness to talk about it. I think I have survived my adoption experience relatively unscathed, but I do have some fears as a direct result of my adoption—one being the intense fear of rejection. When searching for you, I was prepared for the scenario that you wouldn't want to have a relationship. Now that we are trying to establish one, losing you again would be crushing for me. It feels so strange to be saying that as a strong woman! Anyway, I wanted to let you know that I don't enter relationships casually. I can't help but think how much my adoption impacted your life as I know it would mine. I am really looking forward to having you in my life (again).

Love,
Kacie

Now I was sitting on my birth mother's living room couch, listening to the full story of her family dynamics. Moments earlier, we adjourned from the study to rejoin her husband. Walking past the fireplace mantel, I saw framed photos of redheaded babies. "Are these your grandkids?" I asked.

Katherine and her husband met the February after my relinquishment and married that November. She told her soon-to-be husband about me after heeding her mother's warning about bringing secrets into a marriage. Two years after giving birth to me, she had a son. Five years later, their daughter arrived, and then shortly after, another son. Their oldest struggled with mental illness, and he estranged himself from the entire family. Nobody has seen or heard from him in more than fifteen years. Katherine told me that she always had a contentious relationship with her daughter. She was a fiery redhead with a temper to match. She lived only a few miles away, but they hadn't seen each other in two years. Their son recently relocated from North Carolina to Florida. He and his sister were close, and in solidarity, he wasn't speaking to his parents either.

Three kids. All estranged. I tried to process what Katherine was telling me. She seemed so nice and loving. We were hitting it off. I couldn't understand where everything with her children went off the rails. Katherine's side of the simple misunderstanding with her daughter made sense. Why was her daughter being so unreasonable? Why was her daughter preventing Katherine and her husband from seeing their only grandchildren? I was quick to come to my birth mother's defense. I let her shower me with love and praise. I let myself be her favorite, her firstborn, the only daughter she was presently in an active relationship with.

I left our first weekend together on an emotional high. She was no longer Katherine. She was mom. I was no longer Kacie. I was Katherine's daughter. I was in love. I was consumed. I was found.

FOURTEEN

Hi mom,

I wanted to express my thoughts about something, and for me, this would be easier done by email (you are the talker, and I am the writer, I suppose). The subject of your children's estrangement seems to be a recurring topic of our conversations. I know that you are deeply upset by your estrangement, and because of that, I want to be there to support you. But I feel anxious when I think about this issue. I was hoping to address this now so that you know how I feel, and then we can move forward from there. Please know that these are my thoughts and feelings and in no way a criticism of you.

I feel that the estrangement and my coming back into your life are two separate issues that just happen to coincide, but that the lines between the two are becoming blurred. That being said, it would mean a great deal to me if you would reach out to your kids and tell them about me. You have been wonderful about telling your family, and I feel that your kids, my siblings, also have the right to know (and that the information should come from you). However, that doesn't mean that you need to try and reestablish a relationship with them right now. In my opinion, it would be best to avoid any discussion about the estrangement when talking about me. Sending a letter (either mailed or emailed) would avoid any potential conversation about the estrangement that may occur with a phone call. I would be happy to help you craft a letter—having the perspective of both an outsider and your daughter might be helpful. What you decide to do is, of course, ultimately up to you. I will love you regardless. I just can't continue to be a part of the estrangement conversation as I feel like it is not healthy for either of us.

The only void that I have ever felt in my life is not knowing you. Now that you are in my life, I feel complete. So, please don't worry about how other family members (including your kids) may or may not treat me. I am only looking to establish healthy relationships with people who are interested in knowing me—to me, that would just be a bonus. My number one priority is you, and I couldn't be happier now that we have reconnected.

I know that having these conversations is hard, and I want to make sure that we are still okay. I already told you that I wouldn't let you not talk to me, and I mean that! So, I am going to call you again this week just to check in (you can always call me too—morning, afternoon, or evening). I think my fear of acceptance/rejection will be one that I will continue to struggle with my entire life. I just needed to get this off my mind so that when I am in North Carolina next, it can be just about us.

I love you,

Kacie

There weren't many people in my birth mother's life who knew she had a secret kid. When we connected, she excitedly told all the people in her life about me. But because her kids weren't in her life, I was still a mystery to them. I couldn't understand how a cousin knew, but my siblings did not. It didn't sit right with me.

Katherine was the oldest child of five children whose ages spanned almost two decades and two generations. During my first trip to visit Katherine, she told me the story about how her second youngest sister found out about me. She was eight when I was born and seventeen when she learned that her oldest sister had a baby that she gave up for adoption.

Katherine's sister found herself in the same situation as Katherine, an unwed pregnant teenager. The big difference between this sister's story and Katherine's story was that Katherine's sister got to keep her daughter. It was a different time, and Katherine's dad ultimately supported her younger sister's decision to get married while still in high school to start a family.

Katherine came to her sister's wedding in a foul mood. Who could blame her? Her dad forced her to give up her baby, and now he was throwing her sister a wedding. She had to endure watching her pregnant sister, still a baby herself, get married. Katherine couldn't be happy for her sister. Instead of being a helpful bridesmaid, she stomped around with a scowl on her face as if trying to sabotage the entire event. Understandably, the bride-to-be was upset. Why was Katherine trying to ruin her special day?

Katherine's husband later pulled the bride and groom aside to explain, attempting to smooth things over. He told them Katherine's story so that maybe they could understand Katherine's poor behavior. "She can't help herself," he said before apologizing.

This sister was the mother of the cousin who connected me to Katherine. While Katherine's story was meant to be kept secret, Katherine's sister later divulged the story of my existence to her three daughters, the youngest of whom I was now exchanging a flurry of emails and texts.

"Did she tell them yet?" My cousin was worried that news of me would spread fast and get back to Katherine's kids. We both knew that if the information didn't come directly from the source, it would turn the current estrangement into a permanent divide that could never be bridged. So, I asked Katherine to tell her kids about me (at least the youngest two). She called me a few days after receiving my email to tell me that she and her husband had discussed the matter. They decided that they were not going to reach out to their kids. If they chose not to be a part of their lives, they didn't deserve to be a part of mine. I couldn't convince her otherwise, and I was crushed. The loving person I was already head-over-heels about seemed only to be a façade. I could see the cracks forming.

A few days later, my birth mother called me again. "Guess what? Your sister wants to meet you!" She told them. I knew she would.

On a scale of zero to ten, I would rate my nerves at about a nine when I first met my birth mother. In meeting my sister for the first time, I would crank it up to an eleven. This event was about multiple connections—my sister and an opportunity for my birth mother and her husband to end their two-year estrangement with their daughter. The stakes were high, and I didn't want to place my bet. I wanted to meet my sister on my own terms. I wanted this experience to be uniquely ours. But this meeting was set up by my birth mother to coincide with my second trip to North Carolina to visit her.

When my sister walked through the door, I couldn't believe my eyes. I had to look up because she went on for miles. I wasn't sure how a five-foot woman could produce another woman who topped out just under six feet. My sister was beautiful. A redhead with bright blue eyes, she came dressed in something I might wear. We hugged after I threw my hands up and jokingly said, "Surprise!" Katherine quickly stepped between us to embrace the daughter she hadn't seen in two years. I could hear Katherine start to sob. All I could do was stand there and stare as they tried to reconnect. It was uncomfortable.

We finally filed into the living room, and my birth mother didn't protest when my sister sat next to me on the couch. My sister started the conversation by asking, "So, mom, who's the birth father?"

I think my new sister and I are going to be fast friends.

Discover

DISCOVER

January 1972, Katherine

With two missed periods, there was no doubt in her mind. She was pregnant.

She confided in Auntie Barbara, her dad's younger sister, who had gotten pregnant at fifteen and kept the baby. Her aunt tried to talk her into having an abortion. Barbara told her that she had thrown her life away to be a young mother and didn't want Katherine to make the same mistake. While abortions were technically illegal under federal law until 1973, some states allowed abortions under certain circumstances, and they were easy to get. Katherine knew of people in similar situations who had gotten abortions. But Katherine was Catholic and didn't believe in abortion. She also wanted to keep her baby. *I am an adult with a job*, she thought.

Katherine still lived with her parents, and she knew it would be hard to keep her pregnancy a secret from them for very long. Barbara offered to be there for support, and her aunt came over for a visit shortly after their conversation. After the younger kids went off to bed, Katherine, Barbara, and Katherine's parents gathered around the kitchen table. Katherine sat and listened to the idle chatter of family getting caught up while she worked up the nerve to say what needed to be said. She ran her fingers over the burn holes left behind on the Formica, thinking about the night her dad stubbed out his cigarette directly on the tabletop. He had been drinking that night, and tonight, she'd already seen him tip back a few. Katherine got up and walked over to the far side of the kitchen near the back door. She knew her parents would not react well to what she was about to say, and she wanted a quick escape. After taking a deep breath, Katherine said, "I'm pregnant." The kitchen table conversation stopped, and everyone turned to look at her.

"What?" her dad asked, forcing her to repeat the words.

"I'm pregnant," she said again.

Her dad stood up quickly, slamming the back of his legs against the steel-framed vinyl seat, sending it backward. He lurched toward Katherine and put his hands on her shoulders, pushing her back against the door. His face was now so close to hers that she could smell the alcohol on his breath. "How could you do this to me? What is everyone going to think?"

her dad yelled, his spittle landing on her glasses.

Katherine watched as her dad turned to look at Barbara, his hands now loosening their grip on her shoulders. "Did you know about this?" he screamed at his sister. Not waiting for a reply, he seethed, "Of course you did—you let yourself get pregnant too." With her father now focused on someone else, Katherine twisted out of his grasp and went back to the kitchen table to sit down. Her fear turned to anger when she thought about his last comment to her. *Is he seriously worried about appearances?* she thought. Appearances didn't stop him from showing up drunk and getting thrown out of her last theater performance. Appearances never stopped his bad drunken behavior.

Katherine sat across from her mom, who was quietly staring out the window, looking as if she wanted to be anywhere but there. She thought her mom would protect her, but she only sat in silence as her dad pushed her, screamed at her. With her dad and aunt now screaming at each other, Katherine used the opportunity to get her mom's attention. "Mom," she said. Her mom turned and met Katherine's eyes. "Mom," Katherine went on, "I want to keep this baby."

Her dad overheard and shouted, "We are not keeping this baby!" Katherine thought she saw tears well up in her mom's eyes before she stood up and walked away. With her mom now gone, Katherine laid her head on the table and began to sob.

The next morning, no one spoke. Katherine left for work as if nothing had happened the night before. When she got home later that evening, she found her parents sitting at the kitchen table waiting for her. They called her in and told her to sit down. This time her mom took charge of the conversation, telling Katherine that she couldn't keep the baby. The best solution for everyone was to give the baby up for adoption.

"But I want to raise this baby myself. I am an adult, and I have a full-time job," Katherine replied, the retort sounding perfectly logical in her mind.

Her dad broke his silence and asked, "Who is the father? Is he going to do anything to help you?"

"Francis," she said. "I have been dating this guy, Francis, and he is the father."

"Well, unless Francis is going to marry you, you are not keeping that baby," her dad replied.

Katherine's mom put a gentle hand on her arm and asked her daughter if she and Francis had discussed marriage.

January 1972, Francis

"Francis, I'm pregnant." The words spilled out her mouth when they met up at the club on Friday. He couldn't believe it. They had only slept together a couple of times.

"How do you know the baby is mine?" he asked. He didn't want to believe that the baby was his.

Crossing her arms across her chest and doing her click-huff with her mouth, she said, "Jesus Francis. I did the math. Besides, you are the only one I've been with. What are we going to do?"

Katherine convinced him to come over to her house and talk to her parents later that weekend to discuss options. He wanted to do the right thing, be a standup guy, and so, he relented.

Now he found himself sitting in a chair across the table from Katherine and her dad. What he saw on her dad's face made him rethink his plan and make a run for the door. That Friday, Katherine convinced him that marriage was the only right thing to do. Katherine said that if they got married, her parents would let her keep the baby. She really wanted to keep the baby.

Since being ushered through the front door and back to the kitchen, he hadn't said a word. Katherine broke the silence. "Dad," she said, "Francis and I can get married, and we can keep the baby." Before her dad could ask how they intended to support a baby, Katherine finished with, "Francis has a full-time job as a machinist."

"Do you love my daughter?" her dad asked, emphasizing each word with a jab of a finger that was getting dangerously close to his face. Francis wasn't sure what to say. Her dad's hand could be around his throat in a split second. He knew his response mattered.

Did he love her? He was still getting to know her. He resisted the urge to break eye contact and said, "Sir, we haven't been dating that long."

Katherine's dad sat back in his chair, lit a cigarette, took one long puff, and exhaled. "If you don't love my daughter, you shouldn't marry her." He watched Katherine's face redden with anger.

"Francis?" she asked, her eyes urging him to say what she knew he couldn't.

"I'm sorry, Katherine," he said and excused himself.

February 1972, Katherine

Katherine's calls to Francis went unanswered until a week after the encounter with her dad. When he finally picked up, she pleaded with him. "They are going to send me away to Florida!"

She was met with silence and then, "I am not sure what you want from me, Katherine, but I can't help you." Before she could reply, she heard the dial tone of a line gone dead.

With no marriage proposal coming, Katherine's parents decided to send her to stay with an aunt and uncle until the delivery. They told her that she would put the baby up for adoption. It had become clear that she could not return from Florida with a baby in her arms. Trying to put a positive spin on the matter, Katherine's dad told her that there was a military base nearby and that she qualified for free medical care because of his benefits.

Katherine felt defeated and started to second guess her ability to raise a baby on her own. The sexual freedom that had made her feel so powerful only months before now forced her to acquiesce to her parent's demands. She wasn't sure she could handle the consequences of her actions without support.

Katherine pleaded with her mom to reconsider letting her keep the baby. Katherine's baby sister wasn't even a year old, and she reasoned that her mom could watch the two of them together while she was working. "They'll grow up like sisters!" trying to put a positive spin on her proposal, a trait she knew she inherited from her dad.

Her mom was empathic but finally said that if Katherine expected her to raise the baby, her parents needed to adopt the baby formally. She told Katherine that she could probably convince her dad to agree to an adoption but that he would never agree to allow her to keep the baby as an unwed teenager. Katherine was devastated. She didn't want to lose her baby, but she didn't want it to be raised by her parents either. She hated her parents. Why didn't they want to help her? Why did they force Francis to walk away?

August 1972, Katherine

When the day came to give birth, Katherine was all alone. She labored by herself. No one was there to hold her hand through the final stages of delivery. The pain she was experiencing as the baby's head started to crown was quickly replaced with anguish, knowing that this would be the last time she and her baby would be connected. She would no longer be able to hold her stomach and sing to the baby, and in a matter of moments, she would no longer know her baby was okay. Katherine thought she heard the delivery nurse say, "It's a girl!" and she did her best to sit up and look at the tiny crying human covered in guck. Moments later, a warm bundle was placed in her arms. She appreciated the kindness of the hospital staff, even to a girl in her situation. They all knew that she was giving the baby up for adoption, but they were allowing her the opportunity to say hello and goodbye. She looked down and studied the baby's face knowing she had to commit everything about her to memory. As the baby's lips moved, Katherine noticed a dimple on one of her cheeks. She had a curly tuft of red hair on the top of her head. She created something so perfect, and now she had to give it away. Her tears were salty and hot as they fell on the baby's forehead. She remembered her mom once telling her that each of her five babies had their own distinct smell. Katherine lowered her face to the baby and inhaled deeply. The baby was intoxicating, an indescribable sweet scent she wished she could bottle up and take with her. In that moment, she wasn't sure she could hand her baby over and walk away.

She watched—seemingly hovering from above—while the delivery nurse carefully took the baby from her arms. She watched the baby leave the room. Six days later, she signed her rights away. One day after that, she boarded a plane back home. As the wheels touched down on Logan Airport's tarmac, the adoption agency closed her file and sealed that chapter of her life forever.

Katherine was greeted by her mom when she arrived back in Boston. She tried to tell her mom all about the baby, but her mom wasn't listening. "It's too painful," she heard her mom tell her. "I'm sorry, Katherine, I can't." Her contact with the adoption agency social worker now over, and with no one else to talk to, Katherine buried her feelings leaving permanent scars that would never fully heal.

FIFTEEN

I have loved you your whole life, even if you didn't know it—reconnecting with my firstborn is a dream come true.

Sometimes I laugh when I'm uncomfortable. I think it is a trait I share with my birth mother. The stories she'd tell about her father didn't seem funny. He sounded like a jerk. But Katherine's chuckle or nonchalant statements that came with telling me more about him seemingly excused his behavior.

"My dad would call a taxi to bring him to the bar, but they stopped responding because he was an obnoxious drunk. So, my dad started giving the neighbor's address instead and waited behind a bush. When the car arrived, he'd quickly emerge and jump in the back before the driver had a chance to protest. Ha-ha."

"One night, my dad got so drunk that he couldn't remember where he left the car. He came and knocked on my window in the middle of the night and asked my husband to drive him around to find it. Ha-ha."

"My dad and I always argued at the dinner table. My siblings told me just to shut up. I never listened. Oh well."

"In my junior year in high school, three of my friends and I entered the Junior Varieties talent show. We sang songs from the musical *Hair*. We choreographed the entire routine ourselves and got a few of our classmates to accompany us with instruments. My grandmother and mother couldn't believe how good we were. We got a standing ovation from the audience, and we won Star of the Show! When my father finally showed up, drunk, the principal tossed him out before he could see my big moment. Oh well."

Katherine assured me that her father's military career helped to shape her in a good way—that she was outgoing and highly adaptable because of moving every other year. But the story she repeated to me most often was her move from Lebanon, New Hampshire, to Hampton, Virginia, in the eighth grade. She hated relocating, and I think she hated her father for it.

In Lebanon, she developed a lot of friendships. She had her first boyfriend (and still remembers his name). It was a small town which made it easier for her to fit in (even for a girl halfway through her sixth-grade year). She loved her Catholic school and the teachers. Everyone cared. Sister Salvatore noticed that Katherine couldn't see the board and sent a note home telling her parents that she needed glasses. Sister Celeste was young and liked to play with the students. Katherine remembered Sister Celeste pulling her habit between her legs and tucking the skirt over her long rosary beads so that she wouldn't trip during a game of basketball. When it was time to move at the end of the year, the class threw Katherine a going away party and gave her a gift (that she still has five decades later).

Katherine's mother saw the toll all the transitions were having on her adolescent daughter, and she could see that Katherine was happy in Lebanon. Katherine's mother begged her husband to let the family stay behind while he traveled to his next assignment. He refused to listen. "I want my wife with me," he said. So, they moved, again.

Katherine recalled Hampton as being the worst place she had ever moved. It was an upscale community where many girls wore boiled wool skirts and matching sweaters with Etienne Aigner shoes and matching purses. Katherine wore her mom's handmade clothes because that's all they could afford. She didn't fit in.

Katherine's dad mellowed with age, or maybe he didn't drink as much. His youngest kids and his grandkids describe a different guy, someone who was charming and funny. According to some, I would have loved him. Katherine's stories about her mother were always endearing. She painted a tender, intelligent, and creative person—someone who was her dad's opposite. I had a hard time envisioning her parents in a happy relationship. Maybe the marriage started differently. Perhaps his military time and many children brought stress and more drinking. When Katherine's dad passed away, and someone later asked her mom if she would ever marry again, her response was quick, "Why would I want to do that?"

I wondered if Katherine's parents ever thought about me. Were they happy that I was given away to another family? Did that decision spare them the shame they wanted to avoid? Did they feel any guilt for their influence over Katherine?

I found out that Katherine's parents bought a home in Florida in the same city where I was relinquished. It made me wonder if they were hoping to connect with the granddaughter that was never meant to be. They wanted to move before their youngest daughter, Jennifer, began high school. She was only a year older than me, and we would have attended high school together.

I was nearly a Jennifer. It was the name my parents settled on while they waited for a baby girl to adopt. During the middle of their long wait for me, my dad's sister gave birth to a little girl. She was named Jennifer and only lived for nine days before succumbing to a congenital disease.

Fate had a different plan. Katherine's parents postponed their move until Jennifer started college. I would have driven by the house they ultimately bought on my way to school, but I was in college before a chance encounter could take shape. My parents chose a different name for me out of respect for my aunt and uncle. I wouldn't be a Jennifer, and I wouldn't share my high school years with an aunt who shared my name and my DNA.

Would we have connected? Would they have recognized me? Would they have wanted to?

SIXTEEN

Dear mom,

Meeting you has been a true gift. I will forever be thankful for the sacrifices you made to bring me into this world and for letting me back into your life so many years later.

I have been feeling a little unsettled. It's those things left unsaid that are beginning to erode the foundation of our new relationship. I need to be able to ask you the tough questions and get an honest answer. I need to be able to express myself without fear of you getting upset or closing me off. I need these things in order to move forward in a healthy relationship with you…

The Morning After

I didn't sleep. Not one wink. "Who is my birth father?" My birth mother's answer kept me up all night.

We'd only just met minutes earlier, but my sister's first question lobbed from the living room couch didn't surprise me—I am part two people, and she wanted to know the other half as much as I did. After being confronted by the fiery redhead sitting across from her, Katherine crossed her arms tightly, glared directly into the space between her two daughters, and said, "I know who the birth father is, and I am NOT going to tell Kacie or help her find him."

Who is the mystery man? I had gotten nowhere with my birth mother revealing the birth father's last name. She confirmed the first name Francis but never offered any more details. When I pressed, she answered with nonsensical statements. Her favorite, "It was the 70s, and we all slept around." My favorite, "We didn't have to worry about sexually transmitted diseases back then," because I got to point out the other obvious consequence of unprotected sex.

The few family members who knew about Katherine's pregnancy couldn't offer any plausible suspects for a birth father. How could nobody know? The cousin that connected me to my birth mother said that her dad saw a photo of my birth father decades ago and remembered him being tall and skinny. The story of Francis coming to the house armed with a marriage proposal was relayed to me by Katherine's oldest sister—a story she heard from her mother during her decline with late-stage Alzheimer's. "My mom never lied," she told me. Could cognitive decline make you remember things differently? Maybe things you wished had happened to free yourself of guilt before you die?

When I avoided the subject of my birth father, my relationship with my birth mother was good. She was generally fun to be around and showered me with her love and affection. But my birth mother was a contradiction. One of her four children was raised by a family that shared no blood with her, and when I told her that I felt like I had lost part of my identity because I never knew my birth parents, I was stunned by her response. *Your identity was not stripped at birth because it was just the beginning with the wonderful family that adopted you.* I couldn't reconcile her obsession with genealogy with how she wanted me to feel about my identity. If origins were so important, why did she feel compelled to withhold half of mine? And if my identity began at my adoption, why did she feel obliged to give me a folder stuffed with her German family line the moment we first met?

I wasn't the only family secret, and the significance Katherine placed on bloodlines made the irony of what I helped to uncover very hard to miss.

The part of my family genealogy that always resonated with me was my paternal grandmother's German and Irish roots. It was surreal to learn that some of my actual blood originated in Germany and Ireland. My grandmother's German line immigrated to the Philadelphia region in the early 1800s. Katherine's German line also immigrated to the Philadelphia region, only decades earlier. My grandmother's Irish line landed in central Pennsylvania sometime in the early to mid-1800s. Katherine's Irish line immigrated to the United States around 1920 when her grandmother was sent to New York at age sixteen by her parents in hopes of a better life.

Like my birth mother, my grandmother had an unmistakable German maiden name. Growing up, I always felt like I could be a descendant of my grandmother—she was the only person I vaguely resembled. Finding out that our relatives came from the same countries made me feel even more connected to her and the family that raised me.

The curious thing about my DNA is that it doesn't show any German ancestry. The percentage of DNA that should fall somewhere in the Germanic region is instead dedicated to Italy—about 10 to 14%, depending on which consumer DNA platform I use and how it calculates ancestry. This part of my ancestry was not something I gave much thought to until my birth mother's oldest sister asked me to help her figure it out.

I already adored "Auntie." If I struggled to see myself in my birth mother, I chalked it up to being more like her sister. She constantly checked in with me like I imagined a mother would—about my feelings, my life—and our phone conversations could easily stretch to two hours. Shortly after my reunion with my birth mother, she arranged to have me come out for a visit to meet her family. Auntie's family is a tight-knit group. She has three strong-willed, independent daughters and a doting husband. I could easily see myself fitting within their dynamic.

When I submitted my DNA to Ancestry in search of birth family, she was one of two people who appeared on my close family relatives list. I sent two messages, one to the cousin (who quickly responded) and one to her. My aunt took two days to reply, and her response was guarded. I appreciated her desire to protect her sister, and she seemed surprised to hear all of what I had already learned about Katherine once she did reach out.

Auntie is reportedly the glue that holds the family together. It was easy to see that trait in her. My birth mother had once disconnected from her entire family for about eight years. I never got the whole story about what happened—another misunderstanding from what I heard. It took their mother's imminent death to bring Katherine back into the fold. Auntie never held it over Katherine's head. They are as close today as they ever were.

Auntie's DNA revealed results like mine—no German and some Italian. I was eager to help her solve the mystery with one caveat, "Are you sure you want to know?"

SEVETEEN

Here is what I think I know.

I was born to a young, unwed woman named Katherine who gave me away because ~~I wasn't good enough.~~ ~~she wanted her baby to have every possible advantage and opportunity in life.~~ she was forced.

~~It is against~~ Florida Statute 63.162 ~~to disclose identifying information about my birth parents.~~ did not exist when I was adopted.

I am ~~German,~~ Irish, French, and English, and Italian?

Francis, my birth father, sounds like a douche.

I am learning that all families have a good story or two to tell. My grandfather is THE guy who walked uphill, both ways, in the snow to school.

My paternal grandfather died when I was eleven from prostate cancer. His stories of living on the plains of Saskatchewan, Canada, farming wheat were well known. But it wasn't until I read his biography in my late teens that I fully understood how hard that life must have been—living in a small cabin with his parents and two brothers, enduring seasons of poor crops due to drought and dust storms, and watching a tornado destroy the barn that housed their tilled crops. I believe his early experiences made him the resourceful person I knew him to be. When he turned seventeen, he hopped on a train to a better life. He met my grandmother and built a successful grocery business. When he wanted to expand, he did it on handshake deals. He convinced the owner of an empty lot to let him build a supermarket on it. He promised to pay him for the land from the future store's profits. He did the same with material suppliers and grocery wholesalers. The store's grand opening yielded roughly $250,000 in today's dollars—enough to pay everyone back with some leftover to put in the bank.

Nobody knew my grandfather was dying until his final days when he lost too much weight for people not to notice. If my grandmother knew, she kept the secret to herself after his passing. Instead of wallowing in the misery of circumstances he couldn't change, he wrote about his life as a way for us to remember him. He was a great writer for someone who only completed the eighth grade, and his stories captivated me, particularly the one about the journey home from school in the snow (not uphill both ways, but close).

My early school days were not pleasant because of the distance to school and the bitterly cold winters. The one-room schoolhouse was located two miles from our farm and served approximately 30 pupils in grades one to eight. To help my older brother and I get to school, father bought us a quarter horse that had foundered and could only walk. He got her cheap.

We rode her to school bareback the first few months because we couldn't afford a saddle. The biggest challenge was when we fell off the horse. We were too small to get back on by ourselves, and we would sometimes have to walk a half-mile out of our way to find a fence to help us climb back on.

The following school year, father bought us a two-wheeled cart to hitch to the horse. When the school needed a couple of reliable boys to start the morning fire, carry coal and water to the schoolhouse, and sweep the floors after school, my brother and I eagerly volunteered. We used our cart to help, and we were now in business earning ten dollars a month.

One day while finishing up after school, a blizzard started to develop. The winter days were short in Saskatchewan, and dusk was fast approaching. My brother and I unhitched the cart, got on our horse, and started for home right away. It was blistering cold, and the howling wind was only making it colder. Our horse always knew the way home without our help, and our lives now depended on her natural instincts. The snow was falling fast, and we could barely see five feet ahead. When the horse suddenly stopped, we thought she was lost. We couldn't go back to the schoolhouse because the blowing snow had already covered our tracks. But the horse started again. After making a few small turns, we were surprised to see our farmhouse appear. What a relief because frostbite had begun to set in!

I remember once receiving a forwarded chain email (before the invention of social media and memes) that contained a list of reasons why everyone born before 1985 should be dead. We grew up in the days of skates with metal wheels that were attached to our shoes with flimsy straps. Seat beats were a novelty, and small children were allowed to stand in the front bench seat of their parent's car. We were allowed to be free-range—leaving on our bikes in the morning and returning once the streetlights illuminated. And who ever wore a bike helmet? But hearing stories about my grandfather and Katherine's grandmother, who was shipped off to America from Ireland as a young girl, made me think my generation had it good. We were alive because, somehow, our ancestors managed to survive.

Grandma Bridie seemed like a colorful character, and Katherine's description brought her to life. Bridie passed through Ellis Island and stayed with a family sponsor until she met Katherine's grandfather (the German line) and married at eighteen. They settled in the Bronx and had four children.

Katherine recalled being eight when Grandma Bridie ripped open her shirt and flashed Katherine and her cousin as a joke revealing the jagged scars where her breasts had once been. Katherine was so disturbed by the image that she could still describe in graphic detail what she saw. It was only later that she understood the scars to be from a double mastectomy—a required procedure to help save Bridie's life. It didn't work. Two years after the flashing incident, Katherine's grandmother died of breast cancer.

Katherine's father once told her and her siblings that their grandfather had come home one day to find that Grandma Bridie had moved the family across town without telling him. There are some conflicting versions of this story—one that made it seem like an impulsive, sudden decision by Bridie and another that stemmed from Bridie's husband taking off with another woman to California for a time. Whatever the reason, I wasn't convinced that their marriage was a happy one.

Finding my birth family via DNA apparently made me the go-to family expert on genetic genealogy. I was intrigued by the family mystery, and I began to chart out everything I knew about the German-Irish branch of the family tree. What I discovered were discrepancies in the amount of DNA I shared with certain family members. Three of Katherine's cousins were on AncestryDNA, and they appeared on my relatives' list. The amount of DNA (calculated as centimorgans) I shared with each varied—two by an entire family branch. One cousin was correctly identified as a first cousin, once removed. But the other two were calculated as half cousins, once removed.

I pulled some of the closer Italian relatives from my matches and began to chart where they fell on my tree based on their family line and how much DNA we shared. Based on the story of infidelity, the plausible explanation was that Katherine's grandfather had a child from a different line. Or maybe, as Auntie hoped, the discrepancy happened further up the tree. The problem with these theories was that the math didn't add up. Another problem—the four children from Katherine's grandparents all grew up together. They all knew their birth mother to be Bridie. The science all pointed to Bridie.

Katherine's dad was the third child. He and his younger sister were both shorter and darker complected when compared to their two oldest siblings and their parents. The two oldest children appeared legit—fathered by Bridie's husband. The two youngest children had to be fathered by somebody else. It seems that Bridie had a long-term affair with a short Italian guy named Leonard, who also lived in the Bronx. If anyone ever knew, it was never discussed. Bridie took this secret with her to the grave.

Auntie was upset with the discovery—her world now turned upside down. Everything she thought she knew suddenly changed. She was no longer German. Her sixth great-grandfather didn't fight in the Revolutionary War. Her grandfather was someone she had never met. I found myself trying to convince her that nothing had changed—her dad died knowing his true father, the one who raised him, and the one he always called dad. But Auntie didn't want to listen, and I couldn't empathize with her feelings. I was conditioned to believe that blood ties didn't mean anything in my world.

Auntie and I later learned more about Leonard through a cousin on that side of the family. He was a womanizer who fathered several children outside of his marriage. His wife knew about his affairs, and she apparently made him soak his privates in alcohol every time he came home. But she never left. He was the father of her children, and she loved him. Leonard ultimately died an early death in the bed of one of his mistresses. It sounded like a sad life, but it's a life that eventually led to the creation of Auntie, my birth mother, and me. Who could be upset by that?

EIGHTEEN

Hi Auntie,

I hope it is okay that I am sending this to you (I suppose it is too late if not). As you can imagine, I have had a lot on my mind recently. I have always been one to externally process my feelings. I have a feeling you might be the same way—maybe it is a family trait that skipped Katherine.

With an unreturned phone call and unanswered emails, Katherine has made it clear that she is no longer interested in having a relationship with me. I respect her decision, and I am now at a place where I can start to move forward. In the adoption world, the term "mom" is given to the woman who chooses to be in your life. And for that reason, I will no longer be calling Katherine "mom." Please know that my decision to do this is not because I am trying to be hurtful. It is my way of protecting myself from further heartbreak. As an adoptee and a mother to two adopted children, I will never understand her decision to walk away the second time.

Non-adoptees have a hard time understanding the challenges that some adoptees have faced throughout their life. I was placed with an amazing and supportive family, and I wanted for nothing. And yet, there was always an indescribable void in my life.

I would constantly search faces for someone who looked like me. I had this unquenchable desire to know where I came from. Being adopted led to a fear of rejection, separation anxiety issues, and being an overachiever. I was always a people pleaser who was afraid of disappointing others. Meeting Katherine has helped me to make some sense of my life, and I will never regret my decision to search. Maybe if Katherine and I had met 10 or 20 years ago, our story would have a different ending. But I will always be grateful to have had her in my life for the short amount of time she was in it—maybe it was meant to be this way. I have accepted that she will no longer be a part of my life. There is nothing to fix. It is what it is, and I am at peace with this new reality.

I have lived my whole life thinking that I was exactly like my birth mother. I get the sense it was the same for her. But I am not the redhead of her dreams. I remember her facial expression when we first met, intently trying to find some resemblance between the two of us. I think we were both surprised to learn that we are really nothing alike (apart from our adventurous spirit). I tried so hard at the beginning of our relationship to be everything she wanted me to be (refer to the paragraph above about the people-pleasing rejection bit). I did things that were completely out of character. I wanted her to love me, to accept me. It took me a while, but I finally realized that whatever I was able to give would never be enough for her. I felt like she wanted to claim me as her own without having to do any of the work. It started to make me feel uncomfortable. I wish I were in a better place to work on a relationship, but I am emotionally tapped, having watched my own mom's eight-year decline all while trying to raise a very challenging child with special needs.

I felt very conflicted about having a relationship with the extended family if Katherine wasn't a part of it. She once told me that you were "her people." I will never understand how someone so loving most of the time could say such hurtful things at times. But I finally came to realize that you are my people too. I am happy that you want to be a part of my life.

Overall, I view my entry back into Katherine's life as a positive. She was able to see that I had turned into a happy, healthy, and independent woman. Our reunion also seemed to be the catalyst that brought her kids back into her life. I hope that Katherine feels a sense of pride for her sacrifice for me. I have not wasted this life that she gave me. I will always love her.

Love,
Kacie

Limbo

The subject of my birth father's identity was becoming exhausting, and I felt myself starting to pull away. I tried to be understanding. I was patient. But, over time, I realized that she just wanted to start at the point in which I reentered her life. She loved to say, "I always knew you would come back to me."

It wasn't until about five months into our reunion that I

finally realized that our goals were not the same. My birth mother was never going to be fully open with me. It was easy for her to believe that I was okay because I grew up in a great family. Our reunion became about her and her sacrifice, not about me and my needs. I needed to be the child.

As a last-ditch effort, I planned a special getaway weekend with Katherine. We hadn't been truly alone together since meeting, and I was hoping this trip would create an intimate setting without distractions (like a husband listening in). Maybe she'd allow herself to open up about my birth father.

I couldn't figure out what was holding her back. Was it that she wanted me all to herself? She already struggled with my relationship with her sister telling me that everyone loved Auntie more than her. Was she withholding my birth father's last name so that he could be perceived as the bad guy indefinitely? Francis walked away instead of choosing to help. Was she too scarred and angry to even talk? I learned that she shut down over any uncomfortable topic involving her. Or was she just trying to protect me? Her baby was rejected, not only by her dad but also by Francis.

My birth mother was happy that I'd been born, but she appeared wounded by the situation that created me. Why?

Right before our weekend together, I noticed a first cousin match on 23andMe. Until then, my closest family match had been a third cousin, and I hadn't had much success tracking down any helpful information. I had gone from checking my DNA profile weekly to every few months. It had been a while since I had last logged into the ancestry service, and I couldn't be sure how long the match had been sitting on my relatives' list. The name didn't sound like one I had heard before from my birth mother's side of the family, and this new match didn't share any DNA relatives from my birth mother's side of the family. I was hopeful that it might be a connection to my birth father.

I reached out, sending a message through the website.

> *23andMe has matched us as first cousins, and I am interested in learning more about how we might be related. I am a female adoptee who is looking for birth family information. I was born in the summer of 1972, and my birth family was reportedly from, or living in, the Boston area at the time of my birth. Any information you can provide, including any family surnames, would be greatly appreciated. Thanks, Katherine (Kacie).*

I received a reply within an hour, and I smiled when I read, "This is pretty exciting! We share the same name! Katherine & Kathryn!!" She mentioned that she loved genealogy and finding family, and she seemed receptive to helping me solve the mystery. We exchanged a flurry of emails. I gave her all the information I knew, and she gave me all possible surnames from her side of the family and the names of people that may appear in my 23andMe DNA Relatives list. By process of elimination, we had determined that we were connected through her father's side. Kathryn sent me a family tree listing three generations of her paternal relatives, putting me closer than I had ever been to discovering my birth father's last name.

I pressed my birth mother too hard, and I knew she would retreat—her typical modus operandi when she felt pushed into a corner. And for her, it meant not calling. On the last night of our weekend together, I'd carefully broached the topic of my birth father. When I told her that I connected with someone on my birth father's side of the family through DNA, she blurted out Francis' last name before I could even ask the question. The name she gave me was unexpected, and Katherine refused to provide any more details. I walked away that weekend with my birth father's full name and a guilt trip for wanting to know more.

At the very beginning of our relationship, I had cautioned her not to build any walls between us—that I couldn't handle it emotionally. By the time I entered her life, she had estranged so many others from it. Her decision to shut me out was a sign that she was willing to risk it all—another daughter and the relationship she assured me she always wanted.

My email to her was harsh, sent on the heels of a recent phone exchange. I should have waited to cool off, but I was tired of her being the only one who got to have their needs met. Understanding that I might (sometime soon) connect with my birth father started to sink in, and Katherine opened our conversation with, "I am still your priority, right?"

Was she really using my own words against me? Why did I ever make such an impossible promise?

My reactive retort of, "No, actually, my first family is my priority," was met with her, "But, I carried you for nine months!" Then she changed the subject. She must have sensed that the silence on the other end of the line meant I was irritated. I was irritated. And I wrote with my filter removed.

> *...Because of your passive-aggressive way of asking me to prioritize the people in my life, I need to hit the pause button... Your reluctance to talk about my beginnings has ultimately shifted the focus of my journey to you and your feelings... I am not going to tolerate emotional walls or barriers... If you can't say something nice, don't say it—please leave out the drama... You need to acknowledge my beginnings...*

My one last plea was met only with silence.

> *My identity comes from my untold story. When you are ready to open up about the past, I will be here to listen. You will always be my mom, and I will always love you.*

Instead, she called this sister and that cousin to tell them that her relationship with me was over. I was to blame for our falling out. I was a horrible person for wanting more than just her.

Given the amount of DNA I shared with my cousin Kathryn, my birth father had to be someone in the family tree she sent. And if we were indeed first cousins, there were only two suspects. The first was her uncle Vernon, someone she reported as sexually abusing his young brothers and cousins before moving on to his nephews. The second was her uncle Robert who divorced his first wife in 1970 and married his second wife early in 1971. Neither candidate, the pedophile or recently married guy, made the ideal birth father, and both were well older than the reported age of twenty-one in late 1971 when I was conceived.

Kathryn had been baffled by the name Francis. She didn't know anyone in her family with that name—uncle, cousin, or otherwise. I began to wonder if my birth father was someone else's family secret. Was he adopted too?

I tried to remain hopeful, digging into family names and DNA relationships. The amount of DNA that Kathryn and I shared put us in a relationship range of either first cousins or first cousins once removed. Could I be the grandchild of Vernon or Robert? Vernon never married, so my focus turned to Robert's first wife, Ruby. If Robert, Ruby, and I all share DNA, I must come from that family line.

Ruby's last name was too common to confirm a relationship definitively. I went further up the tree. But Ruby's ancestry was challenging to trace. Census data put Ruby and her younger brother with their father on his farm and at an orphanage in 1940. Their mother wasn't listed in the census, but I tracked her down through a death certificate. Five years before Ruby's move to an orphanage, her mother committed suicide by shooting herself in the head. Ruby's father remarried and went on to have three more children.

I was curious to know what happened in 1940. According to records, Ruby's father and his second wife, Una, divorced in early 1940. Una claimed extreme cruelty in the divorce records, where surprisingly, she noted that three minor children, not five, were impacted. It appears that when Una left the marriage, she only brought her biological children with her. The two older children were either taken away by the State due to physical abuse by their father or simply abandoned. Both scenarios were heartbreaking.

The death certificate eventually led me to another family name (also common) and more names further up the branch. Through my cursory research of historical documents, I found enough of Ruby's ancestors to compare our names through other DNA matches. They all fit. I am a descendant of Robert and Ruby. Based on Ruby's age, they were likely my grandparents.

Kathryn confirmed my suspicion when I emailed her a recent photo and, in the message, I jokingly said, "…in case of family resemblance." She responded almost immediately.

"Oh my! You look so much like my cousins from my Uncle Robert!"

Robert and Ruby had five children, four of whom were boys. None were named Francis.

NINETEEN

Before me, the undersigned authority, this day personally appeared Katherine, who, being duly sworn, deposes and says that she is the mother of Baby Girl, an infant; that said infant was born out of lawful wedlock; that this affiant was not a married woman at any time within the 12-month period preceding the birth of said child and has not been a married woman at any time since said 12-month period up to and including the date of this affidavit.

-State of Florida, Affidavit of Mother,
Signed and Notarized August 1972

When I emailed Kathryn a photo of me in November 2017, she must have suspected that her Uncle Robert's oldest son was the birth father. There was no denying our resemblance—our brown ringlet curls and the deep dimples that appeared with our smirk smile. Kathryn suggested that I write her cousin a letter explaining everything and email it to her to print. She offered to hand-deliver it to him and help field any questions.

The letter ended up being a five-page "best of" Kacie. It included a summary of years' worth of accomplishments. I had my top ten best photos, from the cute toddler to the daring snowboarder perched on one of Colorado's peaks. It read more like a resume and included facts such as graduating second in my class, earning a Ph.D. in engineering, being naturally athletic, and scaling Mt. Kilimanjaro. I felt the need to sell myself to a stranger and quite possibly the father who might not know I exist.

Early that December, Kathryn emailed me saying she was heading over to her cousin's house after lunch to meet with him and give him my letter. Said she'd call me later.

She walked in his front door with my letter concealed in a manila folder. An impromptu get-together was not typical, and he seemed suspicious. "He wouldn't take his eyes off the folder," she later told me. Nonetheless, he walked her around his house, showing her the kitchen cabinets he'd built. She talked about her parents and her own house projects. And then she held out the folder and told him he should take a look at what was inside. Kathryn's cousin opened the folder to find my letter and started reading.

Dear Ronny,

I realize that receiving a letter like this may come as a bit of a shock to you, and I am not even sure that you are the intended audience. My name is Katherine (Kacie), and I was adopted as a baby in September 1972.

After reading the first two sentences, Kathryn guessed that her cousin Ronny probably knew where the letter was headed. She watched as he began to look through the photos. Ronny paused on a younger picture of me and said, "That could be my son Matt. She looks just like him." He went on to tell Kathryn that he had been lied to so long ago. He confided in his cousin the story of his girlfriend Lee and how he had gotten her pregnant when she was a senior in high school. "She was sent to Florida to have the baby! I assumed she had an abortion," he told her. He went on to explain that he had no idea that she had the baby and gave it up for adoption. Kathryn was puzzled. She'd already read my letter, and I'd given her a pretty good description of my birth mother, including a photo of her at eighteen. She knew her name was Katherine, not Lee. Kathryn pointed to the part of my letter that had those details prompting Ronny to read on.

He finished the letter and looked up with confusion. He assured his cousin that he didn't know a Katherine. Kathryn explained how DNA works, but Ronny dismissed the topic and talked about how much I looked like him. And he continued to reminisce about Lee. He was getting excited and asked Kathryn what he should do next. His actual words, according to Kathryn, were, "Do I pee in a cup?"

That afternoon, I received an email from Kathryn. "Can I call you and talk about my visit? It'd be easier than writing it all down. What time works for you?" After I got off the phone with Kathryn, I ordered a paternity test. Two days later, the test was off to Ronny along with my collected sample and a pre-paid envelope to ship directly to the lab.

On December 19, I got the results, and I emailed Kathryn. There was no refuting that Ronny was my birth father, the probability of paternity equaled 99.99%. I asked her to call Ronny with the news. She told me later that he got choked up when he found out I was his daughter. He repeated the story of Lee and how he felt lied to so long ago, she relayed, but that he was elated and wanted to give me a big hug. She let me know that he was going to call me soon. And two days later, I heard my birth father's voice for the first time.

There is a real Francis from Essex County, Massachusetts—he was not some made-up character to help fill the blanks in my adoption paperwork. I believe that my birth mother thought he could have been the birth father. I believe that there was some discussion of marriage. I also believe that he was the one to terminate the relationship when he found out she was pregnant. I believe all of this because the information in my adoption records is very specific—where Katherine and Francis met, his age, where he lived, his interests, and his parents' age.

Based on the information included in my files, and today's digital technology, I could track him down and send him a letter explaining my story and what I knew about him.

Dear Francis,

I am not sure how to start this letter, but to say that, I believe you are the Francis that is meant to receive this letter. If not, please accept my apologies (at least it will make for a good story).

My name is Katherine, and I was adopted in September 1972 as a baby. While I believe you to be the alleged birthfather mentioned in my adoption records, DNA connected me to someone else. You are not the birth father.

My intent in reaching out is not to disrupt your life or cause you distress. I can't even be sure if you were ever told about me. But I am hoping you can help me figure out why we were connected so many years ago. I always felt that knowing was better than not knowing. My hope is that by sharing my story, you will be willing to share your story with me—and that we both may find a sense of closure.

I told him that my birth mother was not forthcoming about the details surrounding her pregnancy other than to tell me his name and that I genuinely believed that Katherine thought he was the birth father. I asked if he would be willing to share his story. Why were our lives intertwined?

I guess I wasn't surprised when I didn't get a response. I had lived most of my life not holding Francis in high regard. I tried to be fair and put myself in his shoes. Would I want to be saddled with a child I didn't want and marry a woman I didn't love? Probably not. The truth is, had he not walked away, my life would look very different. Maybe it brought him some relief to hear my words, and I was happy to provide him with his Maury Povich moment.

"Francis, you are NOT the father!"

TWENTY

Hugging you "goodbye" at the airport I didn't want you to leave… I feel so good about our weekend… our similarities. I don't cry often, but I came very close. You are so welcome here. I love you. Thanks for being you.

"Hello," I said when I answered his call. "Hi Kacie, this is Ronny from New Hampshire," he said in a thick New England accent. There was a moment of silence before he went on to say, "I am so happy to have a daughter."

We went on to talk for over an hour about our physical appearances, our interests, and our families. We seemed to have so much in common—careers, athletic pursuits, and a sense of humor. Toward the end of our conversation, he said he remembered more about that evening in Boston. He had been invited to the enlisted men's club by a friend. He met my birth mother there, and they had a one-night encounter. He didn't elaborate on any details, and I didn't press him. It would be another four months before he finally revealed the truth about that night.

Will he like me? It was a question that kept running through my mind. Ronny and I met for the first time on February 3, 2018, at the Manchester Airport. When I arrived, I stepped off the plane and went straight to the restroom. I was nervous. It was ten degrees outside, and I was sweating. We had spoken by phone a few times before my arrival, but that didn't seem to help calm my nerves. I looked at myself in the mirror and fluffed my hair. I lost sleep over what I would wear the first time we met. My birth mother hadn't made any comments about my clothes during my first meeting with her, but I still felt the need to impress this virtual stranger. My physical appearance would be the first thing he'd see.

As I studied my outfit in the mirror, I started to second guess my choice. My blue chambray button-up was already wrinkled from the journey. My nervous, sweaty hands tried to press down as many wrinkles as possible without much success. As I stared at myself in the mirror, I tried to squash the thought that Ronny would hate everything about me. I had lived my life to prove that I was worthy of an existence, and it was silly to think about someone getting hung up over a wrinkled shirt. But I wanted everything to be perfect. The outfit, my hair, me.

I popped a breath mint into my mouth before finally leaving the shelter of the restroom. Manchester has such a small airport, and it took me less than a minute to get to the curb outside baggage claim—our prearranged meeting location. Ronny noticed me as soon as I walked through the sliding glass doors, and he got out of his truck to meet me at the curb. *No way was he 5'8"* like he'd told me in a previous phone conversation. I realized now he must have rounded up from 5'6"-ish. *But to hell with how tall he is.* I was now standing eye-to-eye with someone who looked exactly like me. The resemblance was incredible.

He gave me a big dimpled smile before opening his arms to wrap me in a gigantic hug. His arms seemed to go on for miles, and in them, I felt perfect. We lingered there for a moment, long enough to give airport security a reason to tell us to move it along. When he finally let me go, I looked at him and said, "How does it feel to have a daughter at sixty-four?"

Without skipping a beat, he said, "Better late than never. I always wanted a daughter." At that moment, I knew he was my dad.

During my short weekend visit, I got the chance to meet some of his family, including two new brothers and his father (my grandfather). My last grandparent passed away eight years earlier, and it was surreal to have been gifted another one. Everyone treated me as if I was family. Wasn't I?

I couldn't take my eyes off Ronny for the entire weekend, and I kept apologizing for my constant stare. I had never seen anyone who looked and acted like me. The hazy mystery of me was slowly coming into focus. I was beginning to understand what my dad must feel about being an identical twin. My husband later told me that Ronny and I seemed to move together. When he breathed out, I breathed in. I couldn't get enough of him.

TWENTY-ONE

Hi "daughter,"

What a nice word... what a nice sound to say, "my daughter." 64 years it took for me to say that... to realize that... to absorb something I always thought would never be. You have completed me and my family in ways that I thought would never be. I've always wondered what it would have been like to have had a daughter... to have that missing piece. Now I know.

I have absolutely loved our long conversations. I have never been known to be on the phone for any length of time. All business, to a fault. Not so with you. I'm so at ease talking with you, listening to you, being with you. I think about you all the time. I'm constantly checking the calendar for the next meeting when you are not here.

Forgive me for stealing your words, "I am looking forward to creating our own memories and seeing where this journey takes us. I can never thank you enough for opening your life up to me. Thanks for listening, for sharing, and for reassuring me." I couldn't have said it better. We are a lot alike.

I am amazed at what you've accomplished. Thank you for your persistence... your stubbornness to find answers, and "no quit" attitude that is you. Thank you for finding me. Thank you for being you.

Love you Kacie,
Dad

Persistent. Stubborn. Determined. Driven. It was called many different things over my life—a trait passed to me by my birth father and one that I needed to find my way to him. I imagine that the search journey for many adoptees ends once they find their birth family and that most adoptees don't take the extra step to have their adoption records unsealed. But my search didn't feel finished. My birth mother could not tell me anything about the days following my birth—she only got to see me one time in the delivery room. I felt my records might be the key to unraveling the mystery of my first nine days. To me, loose ends felt unsettling, and I wanted to fill in all the holes in my story. But mostly, I felt entitled to my information, especially now that I knew my birth family.

I mailed off my petition to unseal my adoption records in March 2018 to the circuit court that handled the adoption. Well versed in Florida Statute 63.162 requirements by now, the petition included notarized written authorizations of release from my dad and birth mother and my mom's death certificate. Because I couldn't produce anything from the alleged birth father, who lived only within the files of my adoption record, I included a copy of the paternity results that connected Ronny to me. I received a response from the office of the circuit judge that would be handling my case—Judge Covert. I couldn't miss the irony of his name. With no legal access to my prior identity, my journey for answers felt like a covert operation I'd been running for decades.

The court disclosed that my sealed adoption record existed in two locations—their circuit court and the adoption agency. They determined that their files did not contain any information identifying the birth parents or my original birth certificate, and the court granted immediate access to those records. However, getting my records from the adoption agency required an extra step that felt unnecessary. I needed to schedule a hearing with Judge Covert to determine whether I had good cause to unseal my agency records. Referring to dreaded Florida Statute 63.162(2), the court cited a stipulation that wasn't part of the statute when my records were sealed. I wasn't surprised. The court must allow the adoption agency to approve or deny my request according to the law.

Florida's "good cause" clause prioritizes the adoptee's best interest, but what constitutes a good cause and how the best interests of all parties involved are weighed against one another is not spelled out in the statute. Florida continues to be one of the most restrictive states for adoptees to access their sealed adoption records. When I called the court clerk to schedule my "good cause" hearing with the judge, the clerk could not contain her surprise. She told me that I was only one of a handful of closed adoption cases she knew during her tenure that received a hearing. She couldn't recall one that was successful.

When my court date arrived, I came impeccably dressed, carrying my arsenal of documents. As I sat in the hallway outside of the judge's chambers, waiting for someone to call my name, I thought about how my parents must have sat in the same hallway forty-five years earlier. Not much had changed. It still carried its mid-century vibe with dark walnut paneling and dim fluorescent lights. I looked down the long, dark hallway to see others waiting for their day in court and wondered if they were nervous. Not everyone here would leave happy. *What about me?* There was something about having to plead my case that made me uneasy.

I heard my name after ten minutes of waiting. The officer who ushered me into the judge's chambers smiled broadly, calming me. *Did he know why I was here?* I wish I could have told him how much that smile meant to me, but getting over to the table before my legs gave way to nerves was my sole focus. *Can they hear my heart beating?* My experiences with the court have only been positive, my adoption, my kid's adoptions, and deferred jury duty, but being in court always makes me nervous. It feels like a place where I must perform to be believed.

I imagined walking into a room with the judge seated high on his bench looking down at me. But there was only a single table and Judge Covert was already seated when I entered. He met me with a neutral face when I sat down, and I desperately tried to read. Walking into his chamber, I'd thought I would employ my nervous habit of breaking the tension with humor and begin with a joke about the irony of his name. But the set of his face gave me pause, and I sat down and said nothing. *What if he didn't have a sense of humor?* I didn't want to start off on the wrong foot.

He did all the predictable judge-y things, asking me my name and why I requested a hearing, and then the judge wanted me to tell him my "good cause" story. How do you summarize a forty-five-year-long quest to a person who holds all the power to grant or deny my request? I had to decide at that moment which Cliffs Notes version would move him the most.

I told the judge that I was adopted as an infant in 1973 through closed proceedings, that I recently connected with birth family members, and that all concerned parties are supportive of my request to unseal my records. I told him that in 1998 I received non-identifying information from the agency that facilitated my adoption and that this information sparked a twenty-year journey to find my birth parents. I told him that in June 2017, I connected with my birth mother through the AncestryDNA service. I went on to say that six months later, I met my birth father with the help of 23andMe and a subsequent paternity test that confirmed our relationship. I revealed that the person most likely named in my adoption file as the birth father is incorrect and that my actual birth father didn't know about me until recently.

The judge was listening intently, but his face remained neutral. I knew that I had to go deeper, and I ended with a statement that I had prepared in advance. Trying to keep eye contact and not look down at my notes, I told Judge Covert, "The court might wonder why I am requesting access to my adoption file now that I know the identities of my birth family. I can say I have always had a natural curiosity about where I came from and how I came to be. My file represents both hope and heartbreak, and it is part of my story, part of my history. It is what makes me who I am. It is part of my identity. Access to my file will finally complete the story surrounding my beginnings and my adoption."

When I finally stopped talking, the judge asked me about my reunion with my birth parents. I tried to stop talking after answering, "It's going really well," but found myself going on about all the uncanny similarities between me and my birth father and how close we had already become.

The judge loosened, and I could see a slight smile start to appear. Maybe his grin was because my story was relatable—perhaps he was a father, perhaps a father to a daughter. He told me I had met the "good cause" condition, and he ordered the unsealing of my adoption records. As I stood up to leave, he stood up too and stepped around the table, extending his right hand. Shaking hands, he said, "Your story is very compelling. I wish you all the best." His ruling, his smile, his handshake, his words gave voice to an adopted child who finally got her day in court.

I received the official court order to release my adoption information and forwarded it to the adoption agency. The agency that I was adopted through in 1972 no longer processed adoptions and operated under a new name and mission. They weren't hard to find, thanks to my brother, who had made his first request to the same agency for his non-identifying information a year prior. When the agency's Director of Quality Improvement initially took my request, she was hopeful that there would be a quick turnaround time to get me my court-ordered file. I called when I hadn't heard or received any information after a few weeks. The agency located my file, but they didn't have a way to read it.

Adoption agencies must retain all records by law (or send them to the State in the event of agency closure). I knew this. But I had naïvely thought that files would be both preserved AND retrievable. My record only existed on microfilm—a very stable way to store old paper documents but useless if you don't have the machine to read and print the information. They still had the microfilm, but not the microfilm reader. She said that I was the first person she knew that approached the agency with a court order to unseal their adoption record. It just didn't happen. *We'll never need this clunky thing* may have been the last words the machine heard before being heaved into the dumpster behind the building. I could feel her nervous energy through the phone—she knew the agency had to comply with the order, but she didn't know how it could. Before hanging up the phone, I offered to help problem-solve, my persistent trait naturally kicking in to help save the day. I wasn't going to let a seemingly simple problem prevent me from my information. I worked at a university, and I had seen microfilm readers at the library. I knew they still existed.

A day later, I called the agency back with a few options. The cheapest, take the file to the nearby library with a reader. Another option, send the file to a company that converted the film into digital files. The last, and substantially most expensive option, buy a new machine. But when coming up with a list of options, I wasn't thinking about laws that kept my records under a tight seal. The director realized that there was no way the agency could guarantee the confidentiality of records once they left the property. So, the agency purchased a microfilm reader, and almost a year from my initial petition to the court, I finally had my file.

My experience with adoption file storage uncovered a problem with the sealed records system. How can the court, or the State even, guarantee the protection of these files? If, or when, an adoptee is legally able to access their file, will there be a file to access? When my older brother was finally ready to reach out to the agency for his non-identifying adoption information, it was 2017. His report was laughably scant. It basically assured him that, yes, you were born, and yes, you are human. There was a twenty-year time span between when I received my non-identifying report and my brother's request from the same agency, and my report had considerably more information. The adoption agency likely converted all their files to microfilm. We now know that sometime in that twenty-year period between 1997 and 2017, the agency lost the ability to access the files they were legally bound to retain. The agency likely couldn't read my brother's file, so there was very little to report. The agency should provide a non-identifying information report when requested by the adoptee, but they are not legally bound to do so. The 63.162 statute loophole is the words "when available." My brother didn't get his background information because there was no court order to comply—why invest in an expensive microfilm reader to provide an adoptee with birth family details if you are not legally obligated. There are no checks and balances for adoptees. We are forced to take everyone at their word.

My complete adoption record was more than forty pages. It included agency and court transcripts, legal documents, my parent's adoption application, information about the birth mother and (putative) birth father and their families, and my birth record. It did not include my original birth certificate or the final adoption decree, and I later petitioned the Florida Bureau of Vital Statistics for those documents.

When I received my file, I expected the adoption agency to redact the alleged birth father's last name—they were directed by the court to withhold his last name. He wasn't the birth father, and the court wanted to protect his identity. I understood. What I wasn't expecting were all the redactions of my own family—my older brother, my grandparents, my aunts, and uncles. Technically, these people didn't give their permission to release their names (but technically, they probably never gave their consent to be included in my file in the first place). These people were my family. I grew up with this family. Seeing their names crossed out in my records felt like someone throwing dirt in my face. I wanted a copy of my file to help build my identity, and it felt like the adoption agency and the court had ruled I wasn't worthy of any identity.

The records proved to be a valuable source of information, helping to fill some gaps. When the hospital discharged me at five days old, the adoption agency placed me with a foster family. What happened in my first five days, however, remains a mystery. My birth mother remembers only getting to hold me one time shortly after delivery. It was common practice to give a baby slated for adoption a different name, and I became Cheri Sanford. An alias assured the confidentiality of the closed adoption. And in some cases, it concealed the baby, preventing the birth mother from bonding with her baby. If my birth mother had gone to the hospital nursery, she wouldn't have recognized any names. Instead of being with my birth mother until I left the hospital, I most likely spent those first days languishing in the nursery with only as much human contact as the nurses had time to give.

In her book *The Primal Wound: Understanding the Adopted Child*, Nancy Newton Verrier talks about the wounds left behind in the adopted child after severing the forty-week bond that occurred with the birth mother in utero.[41] Adoption is a traumatic experience that begins with that severed bond. In a span of nine days, I was separated from my birth mother shortly after birth, left virtually alone in a strange place, and then sent to live with two sets of strangers—first a foster family and then my adoptive family. I do not doubt that those first nine days left behind a primal wound, its permanent effect I'll never be able to fully articulate, and scars only visible to me.

Verrier's theory could help explain my seemingly irrational fear of bathroom fans—not all bathroom fans, just one type used in the 1950s, 60s, and 70s. They're stainless steel covered with three large exhaust holes. As someone who doesn't fear much, this never made any sense to me, and it frustrated my parents—especially when it came time for me to become more independent in using public facilities. I had an accident one time when it was no longer appropriate for me to be having accidents. I was around eight and out of range of my parents. I was nearing critical capacity, and the only bathroom around had one of those fans. This fear is so debilitating that when I see this fan (even a photo), I completely freeze and close my eyes. Even today, I cannot go into a bathroom with one of those fans without moral support.

Was my irrational fear tied to those first five unaccounted days? I was born in a mid-century military hospital, and this type of fan almost certainly existed somewhere within its walls. Was it above my nursery bed or on a nearby wall? Is it something that reminds me of the dark, blurry images I would see while all alone? Is this one of those primal wounds? I will never know for sure.

The records documented my birth mother's experience once she arrived in Florida. My heart broke for the young woman described in my file. Her parents sent Katherine to stay with an aunt and uncle in Florida, and she spent the majority of her pregnancy alone. She recalls being lonely because her aunt and uncle both worked, but she has positive memories because she felt supported by them. It was not hard to like Auntie Tilly and her husband. The report described them as a very warm, sensitive, and understanding couple. It went on to say that they treated Katherine as a daughter and that they made every attempt to help her over the rough spots, particularly the first few months when she missed home and her family. The report also noted that her aunt and uncle never pressured Katherine one way or another about adoption.

Katherine contacted the adoption agency in March and was seen twice a month by a social worker until her delivery in August. My birth mother and dad have fond memories of the social worker, Charlotte, when reflecting back on their experience. Thinking about it now, I wonder if this would be considered a conflict of interest for a social worker to represent both the birth and adoptive parents.

When I showed my birth mother the two-page agency transcript, she got upset. Most details were accurate. But as I sat and watched my birth mother read through Charlotte's notes, she got hung up on some of the facts. Where Charlotte wrote, "Katherine decided to place her baby for adoption prior to her arrival in Florida. She was able to talk through in great detail her plans with her parents, who were very supportive of her decision," Katherine responded, "That's not true. They forced me to give my baby away!" When Katherine read, "Even though several of her relatives knew of her pregnancy as did some of her intimate friends, she felt coming to Florida was the best plan; having her relatives made it not only more convenient but more comfortable for Katherine," I could see her face start to get red. "More comfortable for who?" she replied. "Why would I go to Florida to have a baby when I could have stayed home and had my baby in Boston?"

My birth mother's reaction after reading the following statement made me think more about the motivations of the adoption agency and whose best interest they were trying to protect. Charlotte wrote, "The opportunity to meet adoptive mothers was a valuable experience for Katherine. This solidified her thinking about adoption and gave her more support and reassurance of her decision that adoption was in the best interests of her child." To which Katherine replied, "That never happened! I never met any adoptive mothers."

Katherine's responses unnerved me because the adoption agency relayed versions of these statements in my non-identifying information report. The adoption agency gave me the impression that Katherine herself decided to give me up for adoption. I now know that she felt coerced by her parents and that the adoption agency probably didn't help her work through her emotions or other options available to her at that time.

Something that I always wondered was what name my birth mother gave me. When I received my records, the only name to appear was "Baby Girl." I thought my original birth certificate would show something else, but "Baby Girl" was listed again. I asked my birth mother if she had named me, and her response surprised me. "I didn't think I had the right to name you." I was legally her baby when she gave birth, but she felt all her rights were terminated by the adoption agency five months before I was born.

No one ever asked my birth mother what name to put on my birth certificate. I would soon be stripped of any past identity away, and the adoption agency and the hospital staff thought "Baby Girl" was good enough to fill the blank line on my certificate.

TWENTY-TWO

Hi Kacie,

I love getting your letters. I get to see (read) your feelings in ways I don't always understand when we talk. Please write as often as you like. Writing is a great way of communicating when you can't be together in person. I can't wait to see you again. Your smile… your hugs… I know deep down that our relationship will continue to grow. You mean so much to me. In the words of my daughter, "…no amount of time spent with you will ever feel like enough. You are stuck with me…" I love being "stuck" with you. No matter where I am or what I'm doing… when I think of you, I smile. Thank you for being the "icing" on my "cake" of life. I love you Kacie… nothing will ever change that.

Love,
Dad

During my fourth visit, Ronny told me the full details of his night in Boston. I told him my birth mother had been cagy about the subject, telling me either that she couldn't remember or questioned my motives for wanting to know more. Having gotten nowhere with her, I explained to Ronny when we first met that knowing my story was important. He seemed sympathetic to my needs and tried to understand when I explained how these holes in my story impacted my identity. Until that point, he said that he couldn't remember my birth mother and that they had a mutual one-night encounter in the back seat of his Volvo. I took him at his word. I think he wanted to be kind to my birth mother. But I also think he tried to protect himself and maybe even me. Ronny had tried to put that night behind him, and he had never spoken about it to anyone. When I came into his life, I brought that night along with me.

Over four months, my birth father and I had gotten close. He told me that he had never felt so comfortable with someone. I think it was because of our easiness that he finally opened up about that night. When I arrived at his house for my weekend visit, a cardboard box filled with photo albums was on the kitchen counter. He said he just pulled it down from the attic because he thought I might be interested to see family photos.

I eagerly grabbed a handful of albums and settled in at the kitchen peninsula. Flipping through one of the albums from his teen years, I saw a photo of what looked like an old Volvo. "Is this the Volvo where I was created?" I asked. When he told me that it was, I snapped a photo of it with my phone to text to my husband, dad, and two brothers. We all found the fact that I was conceived in the back seat of a Volvo funny and probably influenced my affinity for Scandinavian cars.

That evening after we finished eating dinner, I showed Ronny the text stream of the Volvo that I sent to my family with my caption, "Where the 'magic' happened." He laughed as I held my phone and scrolled down for him to read the messages.

"Nice 'ride' :-)"

"At least they were safe!"

Then he looked up at me, and I could see his demeanor start to shift. "Kacie," he said, "there is something about that evening I need to tell you."

Acknowledge

ACKNOWLEDGE

November 1971, Ronny

"What's going to happen with the baby?" Ray asked as they sat in the club's parking lot. The question hung in the air with the exhaled smoke from Ray's lips. Ronny didn't know what was going to happen to the baby. Sitting back in his seat, his gaze shifted from Ray to the windshield and beyond. He tried to make sense of what happened with Lee. He had been shut out. Part of the problem, he was angry he couldn't be part of the solution. Standing outside the front door during his last visit, her mom didn't invite him in. He was there to talk about options, but her mom wasn't listening. She seemed set on sending her daughter away to stay with family in Florida. To have the baby? To get an abortion? He didn't know. He wanted to help, and he felt helpless. Her mom would no longer speak to him. His girlfriend was no longer allowed to speak to him. And neither looked him in the eyes. His girlfriend was still a minor. What could he do?

Her mom told him to leave and never come back.

Mercifully, Ray took his silence as a cue to move on, and he suggested that they head inside. Ronny watched as Ray extinguished what was left of the joint and put it back in the ashtray before opening the passenger door. When he saw Ray attempt to use the coupe's large dashboard handle to help heave himself out of the low bucket seat, Ronny began to wonder if it was such a good idea that they had just smoked half a joint before heading into the club. Ray was tall with an athletic build, and a high school football injury had landed him on crutches. Ray had little problem sliding down into the coupe's seat only thirty minutes earlier, but his impaired exit was like witnessing a baby take its first steps. Ray clutched the handle in his left hand and both crutches in his right and performed three "shift-turn-resets" before successfully making it to a standing position. As Ray bumped his head on the coupe's roof during the last maneuver, Ronny made sure to stifle the chuckle forming in his throat, not wanting to add to his friend's growing frustration.

Once on his feet, Ray navigated his way around cars and to the entrance handily, as if he'd been using crutches for years instead of weeks. Ronny remembered that Ray's agility was what landed him a coveted spot on their high school football team as a sophomore. The club's doors opened into a large, dimly lit warehouse filled with people and smoke. Along with the locals, Friday nights brought in live music, and Ronny could see crowds of people occupying every table. The pair made their way through the crowd to a round table where Ray's friends were already waiting and waving him over. As Ray made the introductions, Ronny couldn't help but notice how popular his friend had already become. Ray only recently had knee surgery and hadn't been based in Boston all that long, but Ray was outgoing, and he always made friends quickly.

Ronny spent most of the evening talking to a woman sitting at their table when he wasn't talking to Ray. He remembered exchanging names when he and Ray first walked over, but he was never good at remembering them and was too far into a conversation with her to ask without being embarrassed. She was a local girl who frequently came to the club, and he enjoyed his conversation with her. She was intelligent and easy to talk to, but something about her eagerness made him slightly uncomfortable. He wasn't trying to come on to her. He didn't need another complication in his life. He thought about telling the local that he had a girlfriend, but how do you casually slip that into the conversation without sounding like a dink?

A couple of hours into the evening, the high waning, Ronny started to think about the half-smoked joint waiting in the car. He leaned over and asked Ray if he wanted to join him. But not wanting to crutch his way to the car and back, Ray declined. The local overheard Ronny's invitation and stood up. She grabbed his armed and pulled. "Come on," she said. "I'll go with you."

Ronny walked out of the club and in the direction of his car with the local girl in tow. When he drove in earlier that evening, he didn't realize that he had parked right under a streetlamp. Now that it was nearly midnight, the light made his beige coupe glow. He purchased the 1965 Volvo 122 Coupe shortly after graduation. He worked full-time to save up money for college, and he needed a better car to get around. As they approached the car, the local said, "What are you, a thirty-year-old businessman?" The snarky comment about his Volvo made it seem too much of a splurge for an eighteen-year-old.

Ronny opened the coupe's passenger door for the local, and he was surprised when she folded over the seat to get into the back. Ronny assumed that she might be worried about being seen smoking pot on a military base. Thinking no more about it, he followed, leaving the front seat folded so he could shut the coupe's heavy steel door.

Before sitting back, he crouched down, grabbing the driver's seat for leverage to get the joint in the ashtray. His hand almost reached the dashboard when he felt a pull on his back that made him off balance. The local had grabbed his shirt, and he fell back into the seat. She was not interested in smoking. She was interested in him. Before he could say anything, she swung her left leg over his lap, pinning him to the seat. She tousled his hair and looked into his eyes before kissing him on the mouth. Stunned, he didn't move. Her right hand moved from his hair and began its way down his chest and to the top of his jeans. She started to unbuckle his belt. He froze, not knowing what to do. Why couldn't he just say *No*? How had he suddenly become mute? He wasn't interested in what she wanted but was unsure what to do.

He was now in the center of the back seat with his legs stretched out to the front on either side of the stick shift. With his belt undone, the local quickly worked on the button and zipper. He felt powerless to stop her. She recognized that he was not participating and became more aggressive, kissing his lips harder while putting her hand into his pants. When she realized that he was not aroused, she was not amused. "What's the matter with you? Are you gay?" He didn't answer. He still didn't say anything.

He knew that he should use his strength to push her away. He had the power but using it didn't feel right. He heard of men being aggressive toward women, but not the other way around. Who would believe him? He started to think about his girlfriend. He never cheated on Lee, never even thought about it.

His pants and underwear down, resting above his ankles, the local worked her underwear off without his help and was lifting her dress to straddle him again. She grabbed his penis and inserted it inside her. *Is this happening?* he thought before his mind went blank.

"You're a fag, aren't you!?" He heard her say when he came to. She had dismounted and was pulling her underwear back on. Ronny just looked forward, not meeting her eyes. She quickly pulled herself together and leaned over to open the door. She got out of the car without saying another word. She didn't have to—the slam of the coupe's door behind her let him know she was pissed. He watched as she quickly stomped away. Finally free of her, he managed to dress himself and drive home.

He never spoke of that night to anyone. And he never spoke to Ray again.

November 1971, Katherine

She got out of the car and slammed the door, angry that she had not been able to elicit sufficient desire in a man to make all of her feelings of inadequacy disappear. They were having a great time in the club, and he just seemed to check out once they got into the car.

What's the matter with him? Why wasn't he like really hard? They had been drinking in the club, but she knew he wasn't that drunk. *I can't believe I picked up a fag.* Despite the fact that her physical appearance seemed to make her virtually invisible to men most of the time, she compensated with sexually explicit humor and an aggressive personality. Once they realized she was open to an easy lay, most men she hooked up with for the evening couldn't wait to fuck her.

She stomped back to the club, ready to put this night behind her but not quite able to assuage her feelings of not being good enough, pretty enough. She thought this guy really liked her.

December 1971, Ronny

It had been three weeks, and he still hadn't heard from Lee. He had been careful to call when he knew Lee's mom was at work, but his calls went unanswered. Lee had her sister call one day to tell Ronny to pick up some things he left at their mom's house. When he got there, a small box of items had been left out on the front porch. There was no note. He rang the doorbell and nobody came.

Had she heard about what happened in Boston? He couldn't believe he left abruptly that night without saying anything to Ray. So bothered by what had happened in the car, he couldn't even recall the drive home. Dazed for a week, Ronny was still trying to process what exactly happened. Did the local go back into the club and tell Ray she had sex with his friend? Did Ray tell his girlfriend, and did this information get back to Lee? Ronny couldn't think of another reason why Lee wouldn't return his calls. He wished he had talked with Ray before he raced home. He let that thought linger before he finally realized that there was nothing he could say, to Ray or to Lee.

All he wanted now was to know what had been decided about his baby.

December 1971, Katherine

Katherine became suspicious when her period didn't come in December.

During her senior year of high school, Katherine interned with New England Tel and Tel for a work-study program. She liked the money, and when she graduated earlier that year, she accepted a full-time position operating the switchboard for the local military hospital.

Katherine was outgoing, and it wasn't long before she made friends with the other phone operators. Every Friday night, a group would head over to the enlisted men's club at the naval base after work, and Katherine started joining them. On her first evening out, she discovered that some of her work friends made dates over the switchboard with young military men calling out from the base hospital. They would meet up at the club on Fridays when locals were welcome.

Katherine desperately wanted a boyfriend. Her fashion was always on point, but guys in high school never took notice. She made a list in her mind of what guys seemed to want in a girl, and she couldn't check any of the boxes—she was short, somewhat heavy, wore glasses, had curly auburn hair, and was in the drama club. She was intelligent, funny, and friendly, but men didn't seem to look past her physical appearance. She had been on a date before, but it was with a friend who escorted her to prom. Katherine noticed how easy it was for her coworkers to get weekly dates using the veil of a telephone. She started using her charm and wit over the switchboard to set some dates up of her own.

Her parents never sat her down to talk about boys. She was the oldest of five kids, and she was left to figure out the rules of dating on her own. Her dad was absent most of her life. Sure, he sat at the table every night for the family dinner, but he never seemed genuinely interested in her. He was a military man who uprooted the family every few years to take up a post in a new state or a new country. He seemed more interested in his career than her. His military retirement came as Katherine entered high school, and for the first time in her life, she felt a sense of permanence. Katherine hoped that her dad would be more available to her, but he turned to alcohol instead. She never felt good enough for her dad, and she never truly felt the love of a man.

She ended up having sex on the first date she set up over the switchboard that previous summer. Her coworkers were having sex, and she figured that's what everyone was doing. She was seventeen, almost an adult, and dating as an adult meant having sex.

She wasn't always successful at setting up her weekly date in advance, and sometimes Katherine would pick up a guy at the club. She enjoyed the pursuit, being the aggressor. For the first time in her life, she felt powerful, wielding her sexuality for love. It felt good.

January 1972, Ronny

Was Lee sent away? Ronny assumed that Lee went on to have an abortion. She never personally told him what happened to the baby, but a mutual friend, a senior on the school ice hockey team with Lee, didn't remember her being gone for an extended period. If she decided to have the baby, someone would have noticed her absence (or the baby bump). It was a small town, after all.

His feelings of loss for a child he never got a chance to meet were overwhelming. Ronny stuffed this loss deep within himself and tried to move on—the abortion becoming just one more thing that he would never talk about again.

TWENTY-THREE

Did seeing his old Volvo spark a new memory about the night I was conceived? As Ronny looked up from my phone's text stream and told me that there was something he needed to tell me, I tried to think about what more could be said regarding a one-night stand. He went on, "I know how important it is for you to know how you were brought into this world. I have never told anyone this story, but I think you deserve to know."

I put my phone down and looked at him, waiting to hear some slight variation of the story he had been telling me the past few months—that he met my birth mother in a bar, that they were having a good evening, and that then they ended up in the back seat of his Volvo. So why was he nearly in tears?

I was so excited to look through his albums when I arrived that afternoon that I never stopped, even as we ate dinner. I had only seen a couple of photos of him through the years, mostly copies of an original. Ronny kept apologizing for waiting so long to show me—exhuming the dusty box from the attic took him some time. Photo after photo, the resemblance between us left me speechless. His junior and senior high school yearbooks, I found stuffed between two albums, were a testament that we lived parallel lives in separate decades. Everything about us seemed the same, from how we looked to activities and athletics. I wanted to stay in that moment of discovery longer, but I saw the album I was looking through before the Volvo interruption sliding away from me.

Before saying anything more about the night with my birth mother, Ronny put all the albums back in their cardboard container and moved the box further down the counter and out of reach. He wanted my full attention, but he wouldn't meet my eyes. Instead, he stared at the empty countertop between us and told me about that night in Boston and how he felt assaulted.

I am the result of a rape.

He told me that his encounter with Katherine most likely changed the trajectory of his life. Lee decided to have an abortion instead of giving birth to his child.

Ronny had a pregnant girlfriend.

There was another baby.

I sat back on the wooden bar stool and listened, unsure whether I should look at him or follow his lead and look down at the counter. It felt like a much-needed catharsis many years in the making, and I wanted to give him space.

When he finished talking to the Formica, he turned to me and said, "But, look at you! You are perfect! What am I complaining about?" He went on to tell me that he had always wanted a daughter. "You were meant to be!"

Was I meant to be?

I sat there in stunned silence. Not knowing what to say, I leaned over to hug Ronny.

What happened to the other baby—the one he knew about, the one he would have with his girlfriend Lee, the one that was supposed to live? According to Ronny's understanding of what happened with Lee, the fact I exist means that someone else probably doesn't. Did Ronny's sexual encounter with my birth mother lead to Lee's decision to have an abortion? I can't know for sure, but I don't have anything else to replace that part of the narrative. Maybe Lee had already decided to have an abortion without telling Ronny. Maybe Lee never got wind of Ronny's night in Boston. Perhaps Ronny and Lee's baby was not destined to live. Not knowing gnaws at me.

When I got up the following morning, Ronny could sense something was wrong. He wanted to jump right in and talk about what was bothering me. His understanding of my subtle mood changes was surreal, almost as if he knew me as much as I knew me. But I wasn't sure how to articulate what I felt because I couldn't wrap my head around the emotion or the question.

Why am I the one to exist?

I needed to clear my head of the impossible loop that kept replaying. I suggested we take a hike. Hiking was our activity, our way of bonding, our way of getting to know one another as we walked miles over snowy paths and worn granite. It was a sunny, cool day, and the ground had dried enough for us to take the five-mile marshy trail that circled his house. Ronny had been excited to show me this trail, one marked with secrets that only he knew.

When Ronny pointed out the nineteenth-century cemetery about one mile in, I couldn't stop my mind from wandering back to the question of existence. Who were the people buried here?

When we stopped to admire the beauty of a small lake another mile in, my mind was again consumed with trying to make sense of my existence. I asked, "Do you think if that night with my birth mother never happened, my soul would have gone on to live?"

It was an absurd question. Still, I willed Ronny to pop in with a reassuring comment. He only listened intently, seemingly trying to understand. He gave me a big smile and said nothing. We walked on.

"Or if it was Lee's decision to have an abortion and not yours, did my soul need to find a way to you?" Ronny's puzzled expression confirmed that I'd gone too deep to rationalize something that couldn't be rationalized. I was falling down the rabbit hole, and I needed Ronny to grab me and pull me out.

I thought I had completely lost Ronny's interest because he stopped to show me something instead of answering my question. "Look, Kacie," he said. "I want you to see this." It was a second lake, bigger than the first one we had passed but concealed behind some brush. So deep in thought, I would have walked right by. Ronny held back the branches so we could walk through and see the lake from shore to shore. I was in awe that something so vast could be hidden. I would have never known it existed had he not shown me. As we stood looking, I went on,

"What if there could only be one baby, and my soul inhabited the body meant to survive?"

He thought about it for a second, put his arm around me, and simply said, "You are my hidden gem. You, Kacie, were meant to live."

Sometimes I think about all the Kacies that could have been. The soul of Kacie, who went on to live in Ronny and Lee's baby, had Ronny not gone to Boston that one fateful night. The Kacie who Katherine and Francis raised had they gotten married. The Kacie who Katherine's parents raised if she'd allowed them to adopt her baby. The Kacie who Katherine raised if Auntie Tilly had helped her figure out a way to keep the baby. The Kacie who another family raised had her parents pursued the adoption of the available baby boy.

Would we be the same? Would I still be me?

TWENTY-FOUR

Here is what I think I know.

I was born to a young, unwed woman named Katherine, who gave me away because ~~I wasn't good enough.~~ ~~she wanted her baby to have every possible advantage and opportunity in life.~~ she was forced.

~~It is against~~ Florida Statute 63.162 ~~to disclose identifying information about my birth parents.~~ did not exist when I was adopted.

I am ~~German,~~ Irish, French, and English, and Italian~~?~~.

Francis~~, my birth father,~~ sounds like a douche.

My birth father is Ronny.

I am the result of a sexual assault.

It wasn't the beginning I dreamed of hearing. If I could choose my own creation adventure, it would be the one of young passion—stupid and impulsive, not abusive. What does it say about me to be made from that energy?

As repulsed as I was by my birth mother's conduct, I found her silence the most upsetting. I wanted to hear her version of events. That she was young and ignorant. That it was a different time. Anything! I'd like to think I would have listened without judgment. How could a mother choose to say nothing over the maternal instinct to protect her child—not from the truth, but how it gets unpacked?

And why was my birth father unloading on me all at once? His account of the assault, followed immediately by the termination of the baby he seemingly wanted, made me feel inconsequential.

I asked for the whole, unedited version of the story. *Didn't I?* How could I be angry at my birth mother for her behavior or at my birth father for revealing his secret? It is how I exist. But the slowly unfolding story kept shifting, and the sense that I'd find one truth felt more and more elusive the further I journeyed.

When I returned home from my trip that weekend, I told my husband what Ronny said happened in the Volvo. His response was immediate, "Yeah, I can totally see that happening." By then, he had spent enough time with my birth mother to know her personality well. I really wanted to believe my birth father, and part of me imagines that because I can't effectively lie, he can't either. Why would he tell me this story if it wasn't true? The assault story benefited no one now. I was content being the product of a mutual one-night stand in the back seat of his Volvo (a story I was now jokingly telling others), and he had already admitted to me that he was a sexually active teen early on in high school. And, of course, there was Lee and the teen pregnancy.

If the sexual assault had to happen for me to exist, why did I even care? Didn't I try and comfort Auntie about what our lack of German ancestry revealed, that we were descendants of two adulterers? We are the same people. Still, the abrupt change in the narrative—first with the surprise birth father and then the sexual assault accusation—brought questions I had about my identity back into play.

If this is how I was created, how can I be good?

There was something in the way Ronny told the story that made it believable. Most of the details of that night were fuzzy—the time in the bar and his exact interactions with his friend Ray.[42] My birth father's time in the Volvo with my birth mother, however, was painted with so much detail it was as if I was sitting in the front seat watching the scene unfold. His emotion was raw, and the story did not change over the course of our subsequent conversations—not one detail.

I questioned my birth father's motives. "Why," I asked, "if you had a pregnant girlfriend at home, would you bring a strange woman into your car by yourself?" I went on, "If I were your girlfriend, I would be pissed."

Ronny understood why I was probing but said, "It was just the culture back then. I wanted to smoke pot. She wanted to smoke pot. So, we went out to my car to smoke pot."

And the reaction of my birth father didn't make any sense. Why didn't he just say, "Thanks, but no thanks. I am not interested," to my birth mother and get out of the car? To that, he replied, "I was on a military base. If she didn't do what I asked, and the situation escalated to the point that I put my hands on her to physically remove her from my lap, and she got sore by the rejection and reported me, they could have arrested me. Nobody would have believed that I wasn't out for sex."

But Ronny already portrayed himself as a strong, don't-take-no-crap personality type. In the same box that contained photo albums and yearbooks were other memorabilia, such as a police report documenting his assault on a neighbor where Ronny's inciting comment, "Can I help you with something, Michael Jackson?" escalated to a right punch to the neighbor's face.

Ronny could see his angry neighbor following him on foot as he drove down the street to his house. Ronny enjoyed getting under St. Cyr's skin. He purposely sped up and then slowed, forcing his neighbor to emulate what looked like Jackson's signature *Robot* move to keep up. This neighbor, according to Ronny, "was an entitled prick who liked having his ass wiped by his rich parents."

Ronny and St. Cyr had an ongoing feud stemming from the private road they shared with nine other properties. Ronny plowed the road every winter, and most neighbors kicked in some money for his efforts—except the prick St. Cyr who rationalized that because Ronny lived at the end of the road, he had to do it anyway. When St. Cyr decided to put up a gate just past his own property to prevent nonresidents from accessing the road and lake, Ronny had had enough. *He doesn't have the right!* St. Cyr could simply drive into his driveway, but all the other neighbors had to get out of their cars and unlock and open the gate every time they came and went. When Ronny ripped the gate off the hinges and hid it, St. Cyr was furious. He aggressively confronted Ronny and demanded that he re-install the gate. Words were exchanged. A punch was thrown. The police were called.

If Ronny's natural crisis instinct was to fight, why didn't he resort to this tendency when he felt sexually threatened? He froze and did nothing. Freezing is not uncommon in sexual assault cases, and experts describe the reaction as a "fight-or-flight put on hold."[43] I could relate to Ronny's response because it was similar to mine when my soccer coach made inappropriate sexual overtures when I was a teenager. We didn't know what to do because doing anything at the moment didn't lead to a better outcome—for Ronny, it was the thought of being arrested, and for me, it was the thought of getting kicked off my soccer team.

What about Ronny's memory of that night? Memories are fallible. Was my birth father's reconstruction of events even accurate? In a 2019 podcast, psychologist Ayanna Thomas talked about memory and how it reflects our perspective.[44] She said that people would often remember things that are important to them and forget the things that are not important. She went on to say, "The interpretation, 'this couldn't have happened because I would have remembered it,' is an inappropriate interpretation of how memory works." When asked about a recent sexual assault case that made national headlines (a certain supreme court nominee), Dr. Thomas explained that both individuals could well be telling their truthful versions of what they remember about that night—based on what we know about memory, they could each be recalling that night as accurately as they could.

Events that provoke an emotional reaction are more likely to get encoded into the brain. Trauma can increase the likelihood of encoding where the brain holds on to vital details that are especially frightening and sheds the incidental information.[45] This theory could explain Ronny's vivid recall of the Volvo incident and the vaguer details of the entire evening with his friend Ray.

Decoding my full story felt like an essential part of piecing together my identity. The problem was resolving a one-sided account of events. Katherine's silence may well be proof enough of the assault, but I knew that argument would never stand up in the court of public opinion. That became clear when I revealed Ronny's version of that night to one of my birth mother's sisters. She refused to believe him, first by pointing out the mechanics of sex and how a male must be a willing participant, and second by pointing out that her sister would never act in such a way at that time in her life (she, of course, was only twelve and may very well have been oblivious to her older sister's sexual behavior). Still, others didn't believe my conception story. Was this denial because people couldn't believe that something good could be created from something bad? I wanted the truth. I needed validation.

A return letter from Francis could have helped answer two nagging questions. *Why was he listed as the birth father? Was Katherine aggressive?* I wanted Francis to tell me more about Katherine, her behavior, and about that short time in their lives. Was she forceful with him too, or was it just as it had been presented—a short-term mutual affair? I was struggling with the unknown. I had assumed that all the unknowns would be washed away once I met my birth parents, but I was caked with new layers of unknowns—Francis, the sexual assault—and my existence felt muddy. I will probably never be able to answer the Francis question, but what about the assault?

I thought about finding Ray to confirm the details about that night when his friend Ronny would meet a stranger, and the course of my being would be set in motion. But I realized he wouldn't be able to confirm any of the sexual assault allegations. He wasn't there, and he and my birth father never spoke again after that night.

I settled on emailing one of my birth mother's cousins, one I knew Katherine was close to during her teenage years and whose mother helped Katherine tell her parents about the pregnancy.

> *I understand that you and Katherine were in contact when she got pregnant with me—anything you remember from that time would help me put this part of the puzzle together. Was she dating a Francis at that time? Was there some discussion of marriage? Why was she sent to Florida? From my adoption*

paperwork, it appears that her parents gave her a choice to have them raise me, but she refused.

You should know that I don't fault Katherine for any decisions she made at that time. Unfortunately, Katherine has not been very forthcoming about the details of her pregnancy, and that has changed the nature of our relationship. I feel that her story is just as much my story—the one I have been searching for many years to find out. Katherine didn't deny that Francis was my birth father but refused to give me a last name or any details. Through deduction, I know that she couldn't possibly have known who the birth father was when she got pregnant. Why did she name Francis? Having this false information for most of my life was probably more damaging for my perceived sense of identity than not knowing.

My birth mother's cousin didn't recall Katherine having a steady boyfriend, and she'd never heard of Francis or talk of any potential marriage. She said that when my birth mother got pregnant, Katherine confided in her that she'd been sleeping around and had no idea who the father was.

The cousin's reply gave me some dimension to a character that Katherine and adoption records had only developed. She was less guarded than the other relatives that wanted to protect Katherine.

When Katherine got pregnant, she asked my mother for advice. Abortion was a possibility but being Catholic was probably a significant factor in Katherine's decision to have you. Back then, pregnancy out of wedlock was shameful, especially if you were Catholic. Her father was also very hard on her. I'm sure if she kept you, she guessed he would make life doubly difficult for her—criticizing how she was raising you, what she would do with her life, etc. Also, any man she might hope to attract might be turned off by the fact that she got pregnant out of wedlock. What would his family and friends say? Women were slowly gaining rights, but there was still a double standard. It was okay for guys to sleep around, but not women. So she was sent to live with relatives in Florida until she gave birth to avoid family and town gossip. We talked many times over the years about what a difficult decision it was to make, but she hoped her baby would be adopted by a good family who could give her a good life and education. It bothered her very much until she met you.

Katherine has a strong and stubborn personality (as you know). Over the years, she would tell me about falling out with this sister or that friend. At one point, it was her whole family. I could never fully understand how she could just shut people out of her life. She'd let years pass before relenting to reconnect, and it was never by her own initiation. Honestly, it was exhausting talking to her because she never gave me the full story. I needed a scorecard to keep track of who she was and wasn't speaking to!

I always encouraged her to reconcile because life is short, and she was missing out on a lot with her children and family. Of course, I tiptoed my way into the conversation to gently try to get her to see she needed a major attitude adjustment. You couldn't suggest to Katherine that her behavior was self-destructive. She always had to be right. I know she has a lot of repressed problems that she tried to work through during our chats. It always came down to her father and not feeling fully loved by him as opposed to her siblings. However, she always had the utmost love and respect for him.

Two years ago, it was my turn to feel her wrath. One day she called me, mad as hell, to tell me her relationship with you was over. She said it was all your fault and would not open up about what happened. Out of sheer frustration, I calmly told her, "Katherine, what are you doing? You separate from loved ones over and over in your life and regret it when you reconcile." I begged her not to go down that road again. She was so flustered by what I said she just said goodbye and hung up. We haven't spoken in over two years. I've witnessed this behavior in her many times, and I knew enough to stand back. She never could see how her actions hurt so many others, and now you. I will tell you that if she ever did call me, I would welcome her with open, loving arms.

Katherine would, years later, reminisce with her cousin about how she'd slept with so many guys, strangers. She often didn't know their names saying, "Isn't that what we all did back in the hippy days of free love?" The cousin recalled being completely stunned by her comment and her blasé attitude toward sex. The cousin seemed to acknowledge my need to understand my birth mother's behavior because she went on to tell me about an incident that happened the last time she'd seen Katherine.

> *We got together for lunch, and we had a very handsome young waiter. Katherine was practically throwing herself at him, making loud suggestive comments. It was mortifying because all the other diners were watching and listening.*

After making the point that Katherine's antics couldn't be blamed on poor drunken behavior (they weren't drinking), the cousin apologized for saying anything that reflected poorly on Katherine.

> *She is a loving and generous person who just happens to have a lot of unprocessed baggage.*

Ronny's story of assault was probably true, but I have come to accept that I may never know for sure all that happened one night in 1971. Despite her actions, I love my birth mother because whatever happened resulted in me, Kacie—a good person created from something bad.

TWENTY-FIVE

> *The undersigned, Katherine, being the mother of Baby Girl, hereby execute this written surrender of said child for subsequent adoption… the undersigned is hereby permanently deprived of any right to such child, and any right of the undersigned to said child heretofore held by the undersigned is hereby permanently forfeited… the undersigned shall not be entitled to the knowledge at any time hereafter of the whereabouts of said child or the identity or location of any person having adopted said child, nor shall any agent of said Licensed Child placing Agency ever be compelled by any Court to divulge any such information.*
>
> - Surrender of Child, August 1972

Because the 1971 Florida Statute made no promise to any party regarding the protection of personal confidentiality, I was not surprised I didn't find a confidentiality agreement in my sealed records. My file contained only one legal document that referenced confidentiality—it was the witnessed and notarized *Surrender of Child* that was signed by my birth mother six days after giving birth. The document, in simple terms, severed all her rights to me. Permanently.

There was no noted discussion of confidentiality indicated in the file, which contained two transcripts completed by the adoption social worker and documented the birth mother and adoptive parent's interactions with the agency. Neither transcript indicated that individual confidentiality would be expected or maintained—at relinquishment, at adoption, or in the future.

When my birth mother signed the *Surrender of Child*, I am sure she walked away feeling powerless to contact me in the future. The language in the relinquishment document clearly severed her rights to her child, her child's identity, and her child's location. The *Surrender of Child* went a step further to say that the adoption agency would not release any information even when directed by the court.

My birth mother may not have fully understood later changes allowing the release of identifying information with written authorization. I confirmed this with Katherine when I asked her if she ever thought to look for me. She told me that she didn't feel like she had any right to look for me because it was a closed adoption. I received the same response from Auntie who learned about me when she was a young adult. She wanted to search for me, but my birth mother and her parents told her it was a closed adoption and, therefore, impossible. And nobody on my birth mother's side of the family knew about the Florida reunion registry to connect interested parties.

I persistently asked my parents for information throughout childhood, but they always told me there was no information to give me. It was a closed adoption, and their hands were tied. All contact with the agency ended at my adoption. The agency didn't provide post-adoption services, and where to seek future help was never discussed.

My brother connected with his birth parents in 2021. It's a complex story. The lack of non-identifying details provided by the adoption agency in 2017 prompted him to take an AncestryDNA test. His results directly connected him to his birth father, and he reached out to the woman who managed the account. She turned out to be his birth father's wife, who didn't know anything about Jeff. Initially thinking my brother's message was a practical joke, her initial response was cautious. But even she understood the science behind DNA technology and was quickly on board to embrace him. The problem was that my brother's birth father was not interested. He would not acknowledge Jeff or tell him anything about his birth mother. The wife tried to help, but even she couldn't convince her husband to open up. She and Jeff corresponded for a few months before Jeff gave up.

Three months later, I received my sealed records from the adoption agency. The last page in my file was something I didn't recognize, a list of names that didn't match any of my birth family members. As I worked down the list, I noticed a familiar name scribbled in at the bottom. The adoption agency inadvertently misfiled Jeff's paternal birth family tree in my paperwork. In all the agency's efforts to protect confidentiality, this slipped through the cracks.

The agency's admission of never receiving a court order to release a sealed adoption file before mine indicated that they weren't prepared for the possibility. The adoption agency never developed a quality control process to manage confidentiality. If someone had thoroughly examined my file before it went out the door, it would have been evident that the family tree included in my file was not mine. And if they spent a little time looking at the printed microfilm files, they would have noticed that I could read all the redactions when transposed.

With the help of two second cousins in my brother's AncestryDNA relatives' list and the ability to quickly eliminate paternal relatives thanks to the handy family tree provided by the adoption agency, I could track down my brother's birth mother in a matter of a few hours. My brother decided not to reach out. The agency's and birth father's failure to provide information left him skeptical that the experience with his birth mother would lead to a different outcome.

Three years later, my brother received a call from his birth father. He and his birth mother wanted to meet him—together. Unbeknownst to Jeff, his birth parents made a pact never to tell anyone about the baby. As young, naïve teenagers, there was no advance planning—for parenting or adoption. Jeff's birth mother managed to conceal her pregnancy thanks to the invention of the tent dress. Contact with the adoption agency occurred while his birth mother labored in the hospital.

When Jeff reached out, his birth father wasn't sure what to do. It took him some time to summon the courage to track down his high school girlfriend. But he finally did, and they were both excited to meet him.

The information my parents could tell Jeff as a young child was all true. His birth parents were fifteen when they got pregnant. They met in eighth grade and continued dating until their first year in college. His story, journey, and reunion couldn't be more different than the one I experienced, except for a single element—the *Surrender of Child* that they would sign in 1969.

Jeff's birth mother recalled never having the opportunity to hold her son. She was allowed to visit him daily in the nursery, where hospital staff kept Jeff safely behind glass. On day four, after the legal surrender had been made in writing by his young parents, my brother would be gone. His birth parents walked down to the nursery only to find his crib empty.

They both relayed that painful moment to me in vivid detail more than fifty years later. When I asked if they ever thought of looking for their son, they told me they were not allowed. The *Surrender of Child* was signed in the hospital, where the adoption agency told them that they would never see their child again once signed. They were underage. There was no other option presented, so they signed.

TWENTY-SIX

Obituary

Baby Girl was born in a military hospital in Florida. She lived for nine days before slipping away quietly. Baby Girl settled in Florida after traveling there with her mother from Massachusetts in early 1972. Baby Girl's favorite activity was being held by her mother and being soothed by her wonderful singing voice. She looked like her Irish relatives with fair skin and dark curly hair.

Tragically, Baby Girl never got the chance to meet her father before falling victim to F.S. 63.162. Due to the sensitive nature of her passing, a memorial service is not planned. Baby Girl's body was sent offsite to an undisclosed location.

My mom gave me the best presents, not because they were expensive, but because they were thoughtful. It was as if she studied me all year and made a mental note of my needs, interests, and tastes. As different as my mom and I were, her gifts always hit the mark, especially on my birthday.

My best gift was Longlegs, a quilted doll with a moon-like felt face and long, tubular legs that my mom made for me. I think my mom sensed that I needed a type of security blanket while I was alone, especially at night, so she created a doll that was as tall as me. Longlegs became my shield, my protector, and together we battled my childhood anxieties. I took her everywhere, including trips. I was horrified when I had to lay Longlegs on the airport security conveyor to be x-rayed with other luggage, not understanding why she, my loyal companion, couldn't walk through with me. My brothers once used Longlegs as their tug-of-war rope, each grabbing one leg. She ripped in half before either brother could claim victory. My mom made me a replacement which I also named Longlegs. This one still lives, surviving by hiding in my childhood closet.

My mom and dad split birthday duties. My mom handled the gifts, and my dad dealt with the party planning, which mainly consisted of family and a marble cake baked by my grandma. I distinctly remember the year my grandma could not make my cake, and my dad had to improvise the best he could. He presented me with a sad-looking cake he cooked up in the microwave, prepared, and served in a waxed paper pan with uneven globs of chocolate icing spread across the top. His cooking talents didn't extend to the oven, but he tried his best. I can see that now.

My dad is not so good in the gift department either. He had to buy my younger brother's birthday gifts one year because my mom was sick in bed with the flu. Danny has yet to let him live down the surplus of items our dad picked up from the local Radio Shack, including a cheap transistor radio that only played AM stations.

Our dad shines, however, in the celebration of birthdays—never forgetting our special day, announcing it to everyone on the planet, and picking out the best cards.

Still, I never liked my birthday. It was a day that brought disappointment. Who was I supposed to be celebrating? The birth of my former self? Who was that person? Kacie was born on a different day.

My second visit with my birth mother coincided with my forty-fifth birthday, the first birthday we'd spend together since I was born. I reminded her of my birthday in advance of my trip because I wasn't sure she knew the date. She never mentioned it, and I assumed the adoption agency and her parents told her to put the whole unwed pregnancy situation behind her after my birth. Still, I was hoping to recast that event as something positive. It didn't turn out that way—the day came and went with little fanfare and no cake.

Before I boarded the plane to return home, she presented me with an unsealed card and an unwrapped box. Both felt like an afterthought—a mad dash through the house to find something that could pass as a thoughtful acknowledgment of what tied us together. The card only said, "There's one thing that should be part of every birthday… Drinks. Love, Mom." The box held a gold necklace with a heart pendant. My initial feelings of excitement were extinguished when she told me that she always gave away her old jewelry as presents. I was nothing special, just another person deserving of something she no longer needed or wanted.

I left North Carolina the second time with a deep-seated yearning I could never articulate until that moment—the chance to celebrate Baby Girl and acknowledge the loss of her.

The overly simplistic adoption theory that "love will conquer all" does little to fill the void of loss. It is easy to think of my parents as a suitable replacement, or even that parents can be replaceable. My parents were great parents, and they gave me a life only some could dream about. They were not perfect, but I always loved them immensely. I feel blessed that when I was born, my parents were next in line at the adoption agency. I am happy they refused the offer to adopt the little boy and waited for me because I can't envision a different life.

Having my life meant losing a different life, and I was never allowed to grieve what I lost. And as an adult, I cannot reclaim what was lost. Secrecy closed that door forever. My identity was denied through a system that would yield to societal views that have since changed. Adoption laws are not designed to protect the adoptee's best interest throughout her lifetime. I will forever be a child sealed away in a system that never gave me a voice.

TWENTY-SEVEN

Hi dad,

As I got to know you more, I thought I would be okay with seeing you less. But I am finding that the opposite is true. You are such a big part of me, in obvious ways and in ways I can't quite explain because it is hard to put words to an experience that has no vocabulary to explain. We were never supposed to meet. Why invent a language to describe an impossible moment? I am left without words.

You seem to be a natural at having a daughter. I love that we have our own special saying—that when we hugged at the airport after our first weekend together, you said, "thank you for being you," to which I replied, "thank you for making me, me." It felt like our first special dad-daughter moment. My dad and I have a special saying too. When I was younger, he would whisper very quietly in my ear, "I love you," and then I would whisper back (probably not as quietly), "I love you too." As I got older, it morphed into, "You are my favorite daughter," and, "But, I am your only daughter." How lucky am I to have two special dads?!

I can't tell you how happy I am that we share this special, deep connection that is uniquely ours. I must have known that a big piece of me was missing because it is hard to rationalize my intense search otherwise. I am finally anchored. My sadness for all our lost time together is waning. Now I wish we could slow down time—whatever we have left together will never feel like enough. But I am excited to look forward and see what adventure tomorrow brings.

I love you more than my words could ever adequately express.

Your daughter,

Kacie

It felt like I was watching a movie because what was being projected couldn't be real. I settled back in my cushioned seat and watched as the scenes unfolded—two men paddling out on a lake, two men chopping wood together, and two men in front of a fire pit recounting stories of their youth. When they turned their gaze to the transfixed woman staring at them from beyond, they smiled broadly and said in unison, "Kacie, come join us." They walked over to her, each offering a hand to hold. Together, they lifted her out of her chair and walked with her to the water's edge. They stood hand-in-hand and looked across the expansive lake as the sun made its final dip behind the mountain. What was once impossible was now possible—a daughter and her two dads in one scene together.

My two dads met the week I turned forty-seven. We all stayed together at a small lakeside cottage. They shared a daughter, and it seemed natural to have us all share one roof.

They were goofy together, at one point summoning me outside to take a choreographed photo while they attempted to suppress laughter—one dad holding a log, the other dad lined up with his ax overhead, ready to chop it in half. Maybe some would see the symbolism of the scene—trust, faith, or hope? Only the three of us would find that kind of dangerous stupidity funny (because no one ever swung the ax).

I could attribute a specific trait to one particular dad, but seeing them together made all our characteristics blend as if we always shared one roof. For the first time in my life, I could see that I was a product of nurture and nature. My family branch grew from the trunk of both dads.

At the end of our week together, we celebrated my birthday. There was dinner, a cake (store-bought), flowers, and meaningful cards. This birthday was like no other—Baby Girl and Kacie celebrated together.

My story didn't have a beginning. It was as if I had purchased a book that I had always wanted to read, only to open it and find the first chapter ripped out. My life's opening line is intriguing. "Once upon a time, a baby was born when she was nine days old." But there'd always be too many questions looming over the storyline to make the book plausible. *Nobody can be born at nine days old. What happened before?*

Maybe this was the reason why telling my story was a daunting task. There must be a beginning before this beginning.

But once I found the missing chapter, I found myself still struggling with the storytelling. As an adopted person, what identity can I claim? I wasn't naturally part of any equation. Am I really the daughter of Richard and Joyce if I wasn't their birth child? Am I really the daughter of Ronny and Katherine if we'd only just met? I found myself teetering precariously on the edges of my background because I didn't want people to find out I was a phony. I bristle if I am called out specifically as either a birth or an adopted daughter. *Can't I just be a daughter?*

Then it just happened. I found my balance. One day somebody I had just met asked me about my birth family reunion, and I blurted out my entire story without thought. I just needed time to absorb the part of me that was always missing—you can't haphazardly rebind the missing chapter without putting it into the context of an entire book that's already been read. How does it fit in?

My identity is not of someone who was adopted. My identity is not of someone who came from mysterious roots. The journey to answer the question *Who am I* made me realize that I was always Kacie. My adoption and reunion didn't fundamentally change me.

But sometimes, you need the complete manuscript for your story to make sense. Sometimes you must be given the choice to look back in order to move forward.

The knowing has set me free.

~~TWENTY-EIGHT~~ ONE

This is what I know.

I am Kacie.

I am Baby Girl.

I am Cheri Sanford.

I am the child of Ronny and Katherine.

I am the child of Richard and Joyce.

I am the severed branch grafted onto a new tree.

I am the hidden gem revealed.

I am the life that was meant to live.

Francis is a douche.

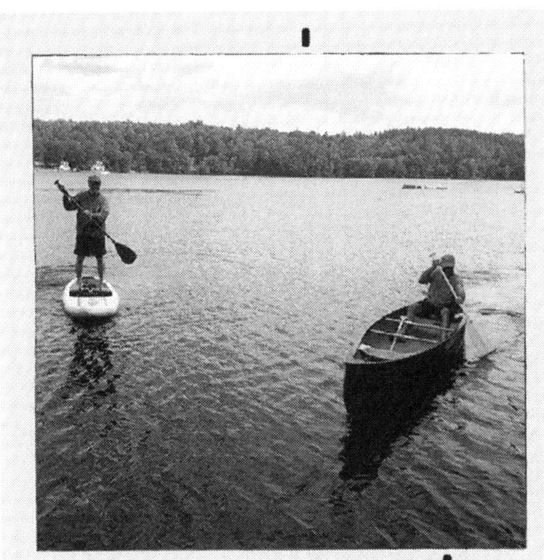

Epilogue

EPILOGUE

Is all *that we see or seem*
But a dream within a dream?

-from "A Dream Within a Dream," 1849
Edgar Allan Poe, writer, poet, orphan

I sit back and watch the light slowly dim. Colors that were once bright red and orange are now gray. Everything is starting to fade into the background. I think I grew up here. I bend over to grab a fistful of sugary sand, only to watch it quickly slide between my fingers. Our time is almost up. I can't hold on. I see your outline off in the distance. I can nearly recognize your face. I call out, but you don't hear me. The light is now gone. Everything has gone dark.

Reconciliation

Two years into the reunion with my birth parents, both would be formally diagnosed with mild forms of dementia. According to family members, they showed signs of memory loss years earlier. But I didn't notice, not at first. I took their repetitive stories as normal for us—people getting caught up on stolen decades.

They progressed to the moderate stage around the same time. My birth mother's dementia is likely genetic. Her mother died of Alzheimer's, and so did her grandmother. I carry one variant gene she passed on to me. My birth father's dementia is likely due to multiple severe concussions—ski racing, pole vaulting—if there were a concussion to be had, he would have participated in that activity.

His worst head injury happened when he hit a moose. He was driving up to Maine in the early morning to start a house build. Having brought his construction trailer up the week before, he decided to take his more comfortable sedan rather than his work truck for the long drive. That decision saved his life. The moose hit the front end and went directly over the top, but not before its body broke through the windshield, clipped my birth father's forehead, and made the roof look like a half-opened sardine can. Ronny was knocked out cold. His car was totaled, but his life was spared. According to police, the moose would have decapitated him if he had been in his much taller truck. He would have died never knowing he had a daughter out there searching for him.

Still, sometimes it's hard to see the bigger picture. *Of course, I meet the daughter I never knew I had and then forget about her only a few years later*, I imagined my birth father saying. I began referring to his luck as the "of course" kind. It would be a trait he passed along to me. Overall, we have had fortunate lives, but neither one has the type of luck that wins you any kind of raffle prize. He'd yell "of course" over any little mishap, such as putting on his boots only to have the shoelace snap or spilling red juice on a favorite gray t-shirt. "Of course!" It would be the end of his life that we finally meet and not the beginning of mine.

I try to hold back my emotions when discussing his cognitive decline, but it isn't always easy.

"You are going to forget who I am. I only exist in your short-term memory, and that's the first to go!"

"Kacie, I am never going to forget you. We have the same smile. I look at you, and I see me."

I try to appreciate every little moment we have together. Ronny is retired and has a lot of time to give. I try to be thankful that we had the opportunity to know one another. I try not to get hung up on all the time we lost. I try.

Our relationship is not perfect, and it has seen its share of bumps. But we have managed to grow together like any father and daughter.

I never fully reconciled with my birth mother. Our relationship entails the annual exchange of Christmas cards and not much else. I wished we could have met much earlier in my life. Maybe our relationship could have evolved into something meaningful. Genetics creates people, and history makes families. But we never got the chance to build our history before Alzheimer's claimed her ability to store new memories. I will slowly fade back into the curly redheaded baby she got to hold once.

I want to thank her for her sacrifice. I want to thank her for letting me go. I want to tell her that I will always love her. But our time has run out. I am too late.

My hope is that all adoptees can access their complete story—before time runs out, before memories fade, before files are lost. As a Florida adoptee, I can't wait to see the demise of F.S. 63.162. Unlike its long, convoluted life, I imagine an obituary that can be summed up in nine simple words:

"Florida Statute 63.162 died. You will not be missed."

ACKNOWLEDGMENTS

Writing this book was a journey within a journey. There are many people to thank, but I want to start by acknowledging my sister, who unknowingly spent her life wearing two sets of shoes. It took a special person to pull that off, and nobody could have worn them better. You are an amazing woman, and I am incredibly grateful to have you in my life finally.

My deepest gratitude goes to all my family and friends for their unconditional love and support. I thank my husband for sharing our life with my pursuit to find birth family and for choosing to come out the other side with me. You are an incredible partner, and your belief in me apparently knows no bounds. For my daughter, never be afraid to let your extraordinary light shine bright. Thank you for sharing your words. For my son, you are a true gift to this world—keep dreaming big. Thank you for turning down your music (over and over again) while I was trying to write. To all my parents who played a role in making me, me, thank you! I think I turned out pretty spectacularly. And to everyone who supported this project, especially those willing to let me write about them, I love you all.

I extend my profound appreciation to a fantastic group of writers at Birth A Book, whose encouragement kept pushing me forward. And a special shout-out goes to Josie Cooke for writing along with me.

Thank you, Robin Locke Monda. Wow! I can only hope that everyone judges this book by its cover.

I couldn't have gotten this book over the finish line without my publishing team, Dorothy Holtermann and Robert Louis Henry. Thank you for your detailed eye, hard work under a tight deadline, and, more importantly, your understanding of the inner workings of LMK (last-minute Katherine)—who blames her pursuit of perfection and last-minute requests on being adopted.

Finally, there is no way I could have written this story without the incredible Clementina Esposito. You are the wizard of your craft. Your magic released the creative writer I always knew was within. My sincerest thanks to you for helping me find my voice.

ENDNOTES

ONE

[1] Naomi Cahn and Jana Singer, "Adoption, Identity, and the Constitution: The Case for Opening Closed Records," *Journal of Constitutional Law* 2, no. 1 (1999): 157.

[2] Karen Wilson-Buterbaugh, *The Baby Scoop Era: Unwed Mothers, Infant Adoption, and Forced Surrender* (Karen Wilson-Buterbaugh, 2017), 35-41.

[3] Ibid.

[4] E. Wayne Carp, "Introduction: A Historical Overview of American Adoption," in *Adoption in America: Historical Perspectives*, ed. E. Wayne Carp (Michigan: University of Michigan Press, 2002), 1-26.

[5] Naomi Cahn and Jana Singer, "Adoption, Identity, and the Constitution: The Case for Opening Closed Records," *Journal of Constitutional Law* 2, no. 1 (1999): 157.

[6] E. Wayne Carp, "Introduction: A Historical Overview of American Adoption," in *Adoption in America: Historical Perspectives*, ed. E. Wayne Carp (Michigan: University of Michigan Press, 2002), 1-26.

[7] Karen Wilson-Buterbaugh, *The Baby Scoop Era: Unwed Mothers, Infant Adoption, and Forced Surrender* (Karen Wilson-Buterbaugh, 2017), 40.

[8] Frances J. Latchford, *Steeped in Blood: Adoption, Identity, and the meaning of Family* (Canada: McGill Queen's University Press, 2019), 7-8.

[9] *Merriam-Webster Dictionary*, s.v. "real," last accessed June 1, 2022, https://www.merriam-webster.com/dictionary/real.

[10] *Merriam-Webster Dictionary*, s.v. "own," last accessed June 1, 2022, https://www.merriam-webster.com/dictionary/own.

[11] Harold D. Grotevant, Nora Dunbar, Julie K. Kohler, and Amy M. Lash Esau, "Adoptive Identity: How Contexts within and beyond the Family Shape Developmental Pathways," *Family Relations* 49, no. 4 (2000): 379–87. http://www.jstor.org/stable/585833. See also Kendra Cherry, "Erik Erikson's Stages of Psychosocial Development," last modified July 18, 2021, https://www.verywellmind.com/erik-eriksons-stages-of-psychosocial-development-2795740.

FOUR

[12] Ann Fessler, *The Girls Who Went Away: The Hidden History of Women Who Surrendered Children for Adoption in the Decades Before Roe v. Wade* (New York: Penguin Books, 2006).

SEVEN

[13] Naomi Cahn and Jana Singer, "Adoption, Identity, and the Constitution: The Case for Opening Closed Records," *Journal of Constitutional Law* 2, no. 1 (1999): 174.

[14] Ibid., 191.

[15] Gregory D. Luce, "A Brief History of Florida Adoptee Rights," *Adoptee Rights Law Center*, last modified February 28, 2021, https://adopteerightslaw.com/report-history-florida-adoptee-rights. See also Gregory D. Luce, "What's at Stake: Florida," last modified February 28, 2021, https://adopteerightslaw.com/whats-at-stake-florida-obc.

[16] Ibid.

[17] Ibid.

[18] Jason Kuhns, "The Sealed Adoption Records Controversy: Breaking Down the Walls of Secrecy," *Golden Gate University Law Review* 24, no. 1 (1994): 261.

[19] Adoption Records Confidential, Florida Statutes, ch. 63, Adoption §§63.181 (1971).

[20] Hearing and Records in Adoption Proceedings: Confidential Nature, Florida Statutes, ch. 63, Adoption §§63.162 (1973).

[21] Hearing and Records in Adoption Proceedings: Confidential Nature, Florida Statutes, ch. 63, Adoption §§63.162 (1978).

[22] Bryn Baffer, "Closed Adoption: An Illusory Promise to Birth Parents and the Changing Landscape of Sealed Adoption Records," *Catholic University Journal of Law and Technology* 28, no. 2 (2020): 154-58.

[23] UNICEF, "The Convention on the Rights of the Child: The children's version," accessed June 1, 2022, https://www.unicef.org/child-rights-convention/convention-text-childrens-version.

[24] Gretchen Sisson, Lauren Ralph, Heather Gould, and Diana Green Foster, "Adoption Decision Making among Women Seeking Abortion," *Womens Health Issues* 27, no. 2 (2017): 136-44, doi: 10.1016/j.whi.2016.11.007.

[25] Lance Bitner-Laird, Dayna Gallagher, Roseana Bess, and Olivia Kenney, "Ensuring the Cradle Won't Fall: Opportunities for Research Related to Private Domestic Infant Adoption in the U.S.," *Mathematica* (2020): 1-7, accessed June 1, 2022, https://www.mathematica.org/publications/ensuring-the-cradle-wont-fall-opportunities-for-research-related-to-private-domestic-infant-adoption.

[26] Xiaojia Ge et al., "Bridging the Divide: Openness in adoption and post-adoption psychosocial adjustment among birth and adoptive parents," *Journal of Family Psychology 22*, no. 4 (2008): 529–40, doi: 10.1037/a0012817.

[27] Department of Health and Human Services, "Open Adoption: Could Open Adoption be the Best Choice for You and Your Baby?": 4-6, accessed June 1, 2022, https://www.childwelfare.gov/pubpdfs/openadoption.pdf.

NINE

[28] Research-China.org, "Orphanage Reliability Analysis," December 7, 2021.

[29] Kay Ann Johnson, *China's Hidden Children: Abandonment, Adoption, and the Human Costs of the One-Child Policy* (Chicago: University of Chicago Press, 2016), 170.

[30] Research-China.org, "Orphanage Reliability Analysis," December 7, 2021.

[31] Barbara Bisantz Raymond, *The Baby Thief: The Untold Story of Georgia Tann, the Baby Seller Who Corrupted Adoption* (New York: Carroll & Graf Publishers, 2007).

[32] Robyn Kagan Harrington, "Georgia Tann: The Mastermind of a Black Market Baby Ring That Lasted for Three Decades," last modified July 24, 2020, https://medium.com/exploring-history/georgia-tann-the-mastermind-of-a-black-market-baby-ring-that-lasted-for-three-decades-f76c8175e4f1.

TEN

[33] Jerome de Groot, "Ancestry.com and the Evolving Nature of Historical Information Companies," The Public Historian 42, no. 1 (2020): 5, doi: https://doi.org/10.1525/tph.2020.42.1.8.

[34] Antonia Regalado, "2017 was the Year Consumer DNA Blew Up," last modified February 12, 2018, https://www.technologyreview.com/2018/02/12/145676/2017-was-the-year-consumer-dna-testing-blew-up.

[35] MyHeritage DNA Quest, accessed June 1, 2022, https://www.dnaquest.org.

[36] Bryn Baffer, "Closed Adoption: An Illusory Promise to Birth Parents and the Changing Landscape of Sealed Adoption Records," *Catholic University Journal of Law and Technology* 28, no. 2 (2020): 147-51.

[37] Ellen Wright Clayton, Barbara J. Evans, James W. Hazel, and Mark A. Rothstein, "The Law of Genetic Privacy: Applications, implications, and limitations," *Journal of Law and the Biosciences* 6, no. 1 (2019): 1-36, doi: https://doi.org/10.1093/jlb/lsz007.

[38] Andrew Perrin, "About Half of Americans are OK with DNA Testing Companies Sharing User Data with Law Enforcement," last modified February 4, 2020, https://www.pewresearch.org/fact-tank/2020/02/04/about-half-of-americans-are-ok-with-dna-testing-companies-sharing-user-data-with-law-enforcement.

[39] Thomas May, Richard M. Lee, and James P. Evans, "Healthcare Challenges Faced by Adopted Persons Lacking Family Health History Information." *Narrative Inquiry in Bioethics* 8, no. 2, (2018): 106, doi:10.1353/nib.2018.0036.

TWELVE

[40] Jean A. S. Strauss, *Birthright: The Guide to Search and Reunion for Adoptees, Birthparents, and Adoptive Parents* (New York: Penguin Books, 1994), 120-27.

TWENTY-ONE

[41] Nancy Newton Verrier, *The Primal Wound Understanding the Adopted Child* (Baltimore: Gateway Press, Inc., 2016), 5-16.

TWENTY-FOUR

[42] Narrative of birth father's night in Boston, in discussion with the author—three separate interviews over a six month period, 2018.

[43] Jim Hopper, "Freezing During Sexual Assault and Harassment: Three brain-based responses, keys to understanding experiences and behaviors," last modified April 3, 2018, https://www.psychologytoday.com/us/blog/sexual-assault-and-the-brain/201804/freezing-during-sexual-assault-and-harassment.

44 Shankar Vedantam and Ayanna Thomas, "Did That Really Happen?," December 16, 2019, in *Hidden Brain* (podcast), produced by NPR, https://hiddenbrain.org/podcast/did-that-really-happen.

45 Rhitu Chatterjee, "How Trauma Affects Memory: Scientists Weigh In On The Kavanaugh Hearing," last modified September 28, 2018, https://www.npr.org/sections/health-shots/2018/09/28/652524372/how-trauma-affects-memory-scientists-weigh-in-on-the-kavanaugh-hearing.

Made in the USA
Middletown, DE
27 September 2022

10910498R00170